United States
Department of
Agriculture

Forest Service

Pacific Northwest
Research Station

General Technical
Report
PNW-GTR-736

December 2007

# Fire Social Science Research–
# Selected Highlights

## Technical Editors

**Armando González-Cabán** is a research economist, Pacific Southwest Research Station, Forest Fire Laboratory, 4955 Canyon Crest Drive, Riverside, CA 92507; **Richard W. Haynes** is a research forester, Pacific Northwest Research Station, Forestry Sciences Laboratory, P.O. Box 3890, Portland, OR 97208; **Sarah McCaffrey** is a research social scientist, Northern Research Station, 1033 University Place, Suite 360, Evanston, IL 60201; **Evan Mercer** is a research economist, Southern Research Station, P.O. Box 12254, Research Triangle Park, NC 27709; and **Alan Watson** is a supervisory research social scientist, Rocky Mountain Research Station, Aldo Leopold Wilderness Research Institute, 790 E Beckwith Avenue, Missoula, MT 59801.

# Abstract

**González-Cabán, Armando; Haynes, Richard W.; McCaffrey, Sarah; Mercer, Evan; Watson, Alan, tech. eds. 2007.** Fire social science research–selected highlights. Gen. Tech. Rep. PNW-GTR-736. Portland, OR: U.S. Department of Agriculture, Forest Service, Pacific Northwest Research Station. 65 p.

Forest Service Research and Development has a long-standing component of social fire science that since 2000 has expanded significantly. Much of this new work focuses on research that will increase understanding of the social and economic issues connected with wildland fire and fuels management. This information can enhance the ability of agencies and communities to meet land management objectives in an effective and efficient manner that is well informed by public needs and preferences. This research will improve fire and fuels management decisions by contributing to a broader understanding of key public values and concerns about fire and fuels management—before, during, and after fire and fuels treatments; social and economic effects of different fire and fuels management decisions; external and internal barriers to effective fire management; and effect of different existing and proposed policies on management options and decision space. The research will also provide guidelines and tools for effective and efficient communication, both external and internal; improving safety, reliability, and ability to meet management objectives; working with communities and other partners to achieve fire and fuels management goals; and assessing tradeoffs in economic, ecological, and quality-of-life values of different decision options.

Keywords: Values, perceptions, suppression, communities, trust, economics, sociology, anthropology, psychology.

# Fire Social Science Research– Selected Highlights

Armando González-Cabán, Richard W. Haynes, Sarah McCaffrey, Evan Mercer, and Alan Watson

Technical Editors

U.S. Department of Agriculture, Forest Service

Pacific Northwest Research Station

General Technical Report PNW-GTR-736

December 2007

# Contents

# Social and Economic Highlights in Response to Wildland Fire and Fuels Research and Development Plan

Richard W. Haynes, Sarah McCaffrey, and Jeff Prestemon

Social science fire research including economics, sociology, geography, and anthropology has always been a part of Forest Service Research and Development but has received increased attention since the advent of the National Fire Plan in 2000. To guide fire research, the Forest Service developed the Wildland Fire and Fuels Research and Development Strategic Plan (see USDA FS 2006). The strategic plan provides broad direction to "conduct research on social and economic dimensions of fire and fuels management" and identifies three broad social science research needs (see table 1 for details). The first deals with "public interactions with fire and fuels management" and includes issues such as public trust, public perceptions, incentives, cooperation and planning, and communication. The second deals with "socioeconomic aspects of fire and fuels management" and includes issues such as assessing values at risk and the social and economic impacts of wildland fire and smoke. The third deals with "organizational effectiveness," which includes issues of decisionmaking, optimal fire management programs, and human factors in fire management.

This document is a progress report on the significant findings from the research conducted by Forest Service Research and Development under the auspices of the National Fire Plan. This is not a catalogue of all work. Instead, it highlights elements of the social science research conducted to date that meets the needs of the National Fire Plan. Additional social science work, not discussed here, is being conducted in other elements of the strategic plan, notably on questions relating to biomass utilization. In some of the highlighted work, partial funding has been provided by the Joint Fire Science Program or from regular appropriations.[1]

Coincidental to the development of the strategic plan, Forest Service Research and Development initiated national peer reviews for eight strategic program areas, one of which is Wildland Fire and Fuels Research. Strategic plan development involves cross-station discussions among the scientists conducting related research.

---

[1] Forest Service Research is typically funded from a single appropriation code. The allocation of funds to specific projects is shifting from local/station control (with Washington office oversight) to local/station/national control as part of the Performance Accountability Reporting Process that is being adopted throughout the Forest Service.

**Table 1—National Fire Plan, Portfolio C-Social Fire Science**

| Element | Description |
|---|---|
| Element C1 | Public interactions with fire and fuels management<br>a. Public trust<br>b. Public perception<br>c. Incentives<br>d. Cooperation and planning<br>e. Education |
| Element C2 | Socioeconomic aspects of fire and fuels management<br>a. Impacts of wildland fire<br>b. Values at risk<br>c. Social and economic impacts of smoke |
| Element C3 | Organizational effectiveness<br>a. Optimal fire management programs<br>b. Human factors in fire management<br>c. Fire management decisionmaking |

In the social sciences, discussions started first among the scientists working on the economic projects and then expanded, in early 2006, to include scientists working on social science projects.

The highlights presented here encapsulate efforts by a cross-station team charged with preparing a summary of social science research for the first National Wildland Fire and Fuels Research peer review. This team was asked to assess and summarize Wildland Fire and Fuels Research accomplishments reported by Forest Service research stations. Central objectives of the team's work were to identify opportunities for cross-station collaboration and to evaluate whether completed research amounted to "integrated systems." A primary product of the team's effort is a synthesis of social science research around 10 central research themes, which we label "highlights." These are described in the next section.

## Selected Significant Highlights

Social science research conducted under the 10 central themes consolidates scientific advances by scientists from different disciplines, multiple research stations, and several universities. Three of these themes focus on assessment methods and understanding of public trust, fire and recreation interactions, and economic and social cost of fire. Two highlights address public perceptions, both those held by individuals and those held by communities. Three highlights characterize advance in our understanding of particular management issues: the feasibility of broad-scale biomass treatments, optimal fire and fuels management, and planning tools for fuel management. One highlight focuses on long-standing work examining the human factors involved in fire management. The last highlight describes research and tool development to produce maps of the wildland-urban interface.

## Literature Cited

**U.S. Department of Agriculture, Forest Service [USDA FS]. 2006.** Wildland fire and fuels research and development strategic plan: meeting the needs of the present, anticipating the needs of the future. Washington, DC. 50 p.

## Assess and Enhance Public Trust

### Highlight Contacts

Patricia Winter, Pacific Southwest Research Station: pwinter@fs.fed.us; James Absher, Pacific Southwest Research Station: jabsher@fs.fed.us; Alan Watson, Rocky Mountain Research Station: awatson@fs.fed.us

### Relation to Strategic Plan

This work supports the objectives in Portfolio C, Element C1: Public interactions with fire and fuels management.

# Background

Trust is a form of social capital, facilitating effective land management, communication and collaboration. Although trust in the Forest Service is at least moderately high for most publics, evidence of a lack of trust and outright distrust has been found in some communities. However, the amount, types, and conditions of trust necessary for effective management to occur remain poorly understood.

# Approach

Researchers initiated studies to assess the degree of trust or distrust various publics hold in the Forest Service's ability to manage fire and fire risk. Studies have focused on describing the level of trust the public has in agency decisionmaking, understanding the constituent elements and contributors to trust, and developing tools to monitor and enhance trust while accomplishing resource management objectives. These studies range from the community level to multistate level, and involve rural, wildland-urban interface (WUI), and urban residents. Combining quantitative and qualitative approaches have been a hallmark of this work.

# Products and Tools

Methods to measure trust and attitudes toward the agency across broad urban public and WUI sectors are being developed. Tools are being developed to model trust issues; quantitatively differentiate segments of rural and WUI communities with high, medium and low trust; understand the contributors to trust; and monitor the effects of public involvement, community-based agency efforts, and collaborative planning activities on trust.

**We have developed tools to enhance trust.**

California Department of Forestry

Effective fire management rests in part on trust between publics and managing agencies.

## Results and Applications

Trust has been found to be centered in perceived values that are similar or dissimilar between agency and publics, as well as perceived consistency or inconsistency of action with those values and validity of reasons underlying inconsistencies (Cvetkovich and Winter 2007). It has been shown to mediate and reinforce the relationship between values and public support for wildland fire management actions such as thinning and prescribed burning (Liljeblad and Borrie 2006; Liljeblad et al., in press; Vaske et al. 2007). However, more work is needed to understand the role trust plays in natural resource decisions, and how trust is lost and gained. Some of the basic tenets of trustworthiness (credibility, honesty, similarity) may or may not be the best foci of agency members seeking to build trust. The importance of trust has been demonstrated concerning reliance on, and likelihood of taking action on, information provided by National Predictive Services. Findings from this will be used to make strategic decisions about communication with various segments of the fire management community in the federal and nonfederal sectors.

The Bitterroot Ecosystem Management Project has assessed trust across communities to understand baseline levels of trust, engaged the public in geographic information system-based values mapping activities to understand the relationship between the public and the Bitterroot National Forest, and will perform postdecision and postimplementation trust monitoring measurements. On the Lewis and Clark National Forest, scientists provided an analysis of the relationship between trust and the principles of high-reliability organizing during public collaboration on a plan for prescribed fire. In Colorado and southern California, results have helped local agencies understand trust issues for WUI residents and assisted community-based fire preparedness communications (e.g., FireWise and Fire Safe Council work, Absher et al. 2006, Cvetkovich and Winter 2007).

## Principal Investigators

James Absher, jabsher@fs.fed.us: Pacific Southwest Research Station; Sarah McCaffrey, smcaffrey@fs.fed.us: Northern Research Station; Alan Watson, awatson@fs.fed.us: Rocky Mountain Research Station; Patricia Winter, pwinter@fs.fed.us: Pacific Southwest Research Station

## Key Partners

Colorado State University, Confederated Salish and Kootenai Tribes of Montana, Forest Service Northern Region: Bitterroot National Forest and Lewis and Clark National Forest, Fort Lewis College, Michigan State University, National Predictive Services, University of Florida, University of Minnesota, University of Montana, Western Washington University

## Funding

This research was supported by the National Fire Plan, Joint Fire Science Program, National Predictive Services Group, and the Bitterroot Ecosystem Management Research Project.

## Literature Cited

**Absher, J.D.; Vaske, J.J.; Bright, A.D.; Don Carlos, A. 2006**. Effective communication about wildfire management along the Colorado Front Range. In: Decker, D.; Lardner, M., comps. Proceedings of the third international fire ecology and management congress. Pullman, WA: Washington State University. [DVD, track 2, community wildfire management]. www.emmps.wsu.edu/2006firecongressproceedings. (May 29, 2007).

**Cvetkovich, G.T.; Winter, P.L. 2007**. The what, how, and when of social reliance and cooperative risk management. In: Siegrist, M.; Earle, T.C.; Gutscher, H., eds. Trust in cooperative risk management: uncertainty and skepticism in the public mind. London: Earthscan: 187–209.

**Liljeblad, A.; Borrie, W.T. 2006**. Trust in wildland fire and fuel management decisions. International Journal of Wilderness. 12(1): 39–43.

**Liljeblad, A.; Watson, A.E.; Borrie, W.T. [In press]**. A look inside the dynamics of trust: a guide for managers. In: Watson, A.; Sproull, J.; Dean, L., comps. Science and stewardship to protect and sustain wilderness values: 8th world wilderness congress symposium; 2005. Proceedings. Fort Collins, CO: U.S. Department of Agriculture, Forest Service, Rocky Mountain Research Station.

**Vaske, J.J.; Absher, J.D.; Bright, A.D. 2007**. Salient value similarity, social trust and attitudes toward wildland fire management strategies. Human Ecology Review. 14(2): 217–226.

## Additional Readings

**Cvetkovich, G.T.; Winter, P.L. 2004.** Seeing eye-to-eye on natural resource management: trust, value similarity, and action consistency/justification. In: Tierney, P.T.; Chavez, D.J., tech. coords. Proceedings of the 4th social aspects and recreation research symposium. San Francisco: San Francisco State University: 46–50.

**Knotek, K. 2005.** Human aspects of fire and fuels management in the Northern Rockies. Eco-Report (Fall 2005). Missoula, MT: U.S. Department of Agriculture, Forest Service, Rocky Mountain Research Station, Bitterroot Ecosystem Management Research Project, Leopold Institute. 573: 9.

**Liljeblad, A. 2005.** Towards a comprehensive definition of trust: understanding the public's trust in natural resource management. Missoula, MT: The University of Montana. 112 p. M.S. thesis.

**Winter, G.; Vogt, C.; McCaffrey, S. 2004.** Examining social trust in fuels management strategies. Journal of Forestry. 120(6): 8–15.

**Winter, P.L. 2003.** Californians' opinions on wildland and wilderness fire management. In: Jakes, P.J., comp. Homeowners, communities, and wildfire: science findings from the National Fire Plan. Proceedings of the 9th international symposium on society and resource management. Gen. Tech. Rep. NC-231. St. Paul, MN: U.S. Department of Agriculture, Forest Service, North Central Research Station: 84–92.

**Winter, P.L. 2006.** Urban proximate wilderness visitors' preferences for fire management. In: Decker, D.; Lardner, M., comps. Proceedings of the 3rd international fire ecology and management congress. Pullman, WA: Washington State University. www.emmps.wsu.edu/2006firecongressproceedings/Changes/PatWinter.pdf. (May 29, 2007).

**Winter, P.L.; Bigler-Cole, H. 2006.** Improving a national fire information program: a needs assessment approach. Proceedings of the 3rd international fire ecology and management congress. [DVD, track 2, public perception]. www.emmps.wsu.edu/2006firecongressproceedings. (May 9, 2007).

**Winter, P.L.; Bigler-Cole, H. [In press].** Information needs, tolerance for risk, and protection from risk: the case of national predictive services customers. In: Beatty, J.J.; Lee, D.C.; Pye, J.M.; Sands, Y., eds. Proceedings on advances in threat assessment and their application to forest and rangeland management conference. Gen. Tech. Rep. Asheville, NC: U.S. Department of Agriculture, Forest Service, Southern Research Station. http://forestencyclopedia.net. (May 9, 2007).

**Winter, P.L.; Cvetkovich, G.T. [In press a].** Diversity in southwesterners' views of Forest Service fire management. In: Martin, W.E.; Raish, C.; Kent, B., eds. Wildfire and fuels management: risk and human reaction. Washington, DC: Resources for the Future.

**Winter, P.L.; Cvetkovich, G.T. [In press b].** Perceptions, impacts, actions, shared values, and trust: the experience of community residents in a fire-prone ecosystem. In: Beatty, J.J.; Lee, D.C.; Pye, J.M.; Sands, Y., eds. Proceedings on advances in threat assessment and their application to forest and rangeland management conference. Gen. Tech. Rep. Asheville, NC: U.S. Department of Agriculture, Forest Service, Southern Research Station. http://forestencyclopedia.net. (May 9, 2007).

# Assess and Understand the Interaction of Fire and Recreation

## Highlight Contacts

Patricia Winter, Pacific Southwest Research Station: pwinter@fs.fed.us

## Relation to Strategic Plan

This work supports the objectives in Portfolio C, Element C1: Public interactions with fire and fuels management.

# Background

Recreation and tourism connected to our national forests have significant interactions with fire and fuels management. Substantial research has been conducted in recent years within this topical area. Among the specific study topics examined is the impact of fire and fuels management upon visitor experiences. These studies help inform management, communication, and education efforts.

# Approach

Varied approaches are characteristic of the inquiry into the relationship between fire and fuels management and recreation. Ranging from a specific recreation area or forest to a multistate level, these studies have involved recreationists and tourists visiting semideveloped sites, trails, and wilderness. Perspectives of the general public have been gathered through onsite, mailed, and telephone surveys and analyses of preexisting records.

# Products and Tools

Findings from a travel cost analysis of 182,987 wilderness recreation permits that span more than a decade are now available. Specific management actions were examined for public acceptability, both from the recreationist and broader public perspectives, and these findings have been repeatedly shared with fire and recreation managers. Multiple scales and measurement approaches have been developed and refined, helping to advance inquiries in this topical area.

## Results and Applications

Investigations into the way that recreationists think about and act in relation to wildland and wilderness fires have been examined. Studies conducted with visitors to wilderness areas in Washington, Oregon, California, Idaho, and Montana indicate that visitor attitudes toward the use of wildland fire in wilderness have changed over the past 40 years. In all cases, visitor attitudes have become more positive and supportive. This trend was consistent across wilderness areas, methods of visitor sampling, and attitude metrics (Knotek 2006).

Inquiries about recreation-related fire management actions have shown lesser support for exclusion of specific recreational uses than for closures of sites and larger forest areas (Winter 2006; Winter and Cvetkovich 2003, in press). Broader fire management actions and policies (e.g., forest health/thinning and prescribed burns) have also been examined in combination with various elements (such as beliefs, trust, and ignition source) Absher and Vaske 2006; Bright et al. 2005; Kneeshaw et al. 2004a, 2004b). A cognitive hierarchy framework has been applied to this work, and new scales have been developed to assess value-based beliefs and social norms. Openness to change regarding opinions or behaviors and degree of persuasiveness of messages has been illuminated through studies on ipsativity in wildland fire attitudes (Absher et al. 2006).

Perceived impacts of fire are also of interest. Tourists have reported that the presence of high fire danger conditions, reported health problems from smoke and ash, and the spread of fire to a nearby vacation region might result in substantial trip alterations, yet most reported that wildland fires would not keep them from traveling (Thapa et al. 2004). Recreationists with greater place attachment were found to have observed more fire-related impacts, and were more likely to anticipate an influence on the quality of their recreational experience (Hendricks et al. 2003).

Actual impacts of fire have been studied. During a high-fire year on the Bob Marshall Wilderness, visitors adapted to the presence of fires by staying fewer nights in the wilderness, were more likely to hike than to travel by stock, and were less likely to fish and/or use outfitters than visitors in a lower fire year (Borrie et al. 2006). Visitation and annual recreation benefits decreased for hikers and mountain bikers as areas recovered from prescribed burns (Hesseln et al. 2003). However, wildland fires had a different impact depending on use, where value per trip increased for hikers but decreased for mountain bikers when crown fires were considered (Loomis et al. 2001). Recreation users should not be expected to react

**Place-specific recreation has more fire-related impacts than other types of recreation activities.**

similarly to fire across activities. Size and extent of burns also affect visitation where increases in the amount of area burned and amount of burn that could be seen from trails are associated with greater declines in recreation demand (Hesseln et al. 2004).

Analyses of burned area emergency reports revealed numerous direct impacts to hiking trails and campgrounds from fires (from fire damage), and many potential impacts to roads and hiking trails (tend to be linked to flooding after the fire event). Most impacts represented a loss of recreational opportunities (Chavez and McCollum 2004). Impacts of fire on recreational values follows a path demonstrating a short-term increase in visitation following a fire, then a decrease in use for several years following a fire, with this downward slope shifting to an increase as the forest canopy closes and the area begins to look like a mature forest again (Englin et al. 2001, in press). Other work showed that the costs of fire can be reduced through prescribed burning, which lessens the impact of lost recreation visitor days due to closures.[2]

On the Bitterroot National Forest, where the majority of recreation visitors are local residents, studies are helping managers and planners interact with the public in a meaningful way in analyzing alternative fuel treatment locations and strategies; and in understanding cultural differences in relationships with wilderness in order to anticipate differences in response to proposed fuel treatments (Gunderson and Watson 2006). Findings from the work in the Southwest were incorporated into forest plan revision for the four southern California national forests and informed a public fire education program developed by the San Bernardino National Forest Association (Winter and Cvetkovich 2003).

## Principal Investigators

James Absher, jabsher@fs.fed.us; Deborah Chavez, dchavez@fs.fed.us; Armando González-Cabán, agonzalezcaban@fs.fed.us; Patricia Winter, pwinter@fs.fed.us: Pacific Southwest Research Station; Tom Holmes, tholmes@fs.fed.us: Southern Research Station; Alan Watson, awatson@fs.fed.us: Aldo Leopold Wilderness Research Institute and the Bitterroot Ecosystem Management Research Project

---

[2] González-Cabán, A.; Wohlgemuth, P.; Loomis, J.B.; Weise, D.R. 2004. Costs and benefits of reducing sediment production from wildfires through prescribed burning: the Kinneloa fire case study. Proceedings, the 2nd international symposium on fire and economics, planning and policy: a global vision. Unpublished document. On file with: USDA Forest Service, Pacific Southwest Research Station, 4955 Canyon Crest Drive, Riverside, CA 92507.

## Key Partners

Bitterroot Ecosystem Management Research Project; California Polytechnic State University, San Luis Obispo; Colorado State University; Confederated Salish and Kootenai Tribes of Montana; The University of Leeds, United Kingdom; University of Florida; University of Montana Wilderness Institute; University of Nevada, Reno; Western Washington University

## Funding

This research was supported by the National Fire Plan, the Joint Fire Sciences Program, and the Bitterroot Ecosystem Management Research Project.

## Literature Cited

**Absher, J.D.; Vaske, J.J. 2006.** Predicting wildland fire policy support. In: Reynolds, K.M., ed. Gen. Tech. Rep. PNW-GTR-688. [CD-ROM]. Portland, OR: U.S. Department of Agriculture, Forest Service, Pacific Northwest Research Station.

**Absher, J.D.; Vaske, J.J.; Bright, A.D.; Donnelley, M.P. 2006.** Ipsative crystallization effects on wildland fire attitude—policy support models. Society and Natural Resources. 19: 381–392.

**Borrie, W.T.; McCool, S.F.; Whitmore, J.G. 2006.** Wildland fire effects on visits and visitors to the Bob Marshall Wilderness Complex. International Journal of Wilderness. 12: 1.

**Bright, A.D.; Vaske, J.J.; Kneeshaw, K.; Absher, J.D. 2005.** Scale development of wildfire management basic beliefs. Australasian Parks and Leisure. 8(2): 44–48.

**Chavez, D.J.; McCollum, D. 2004.** Using BAER reports to investigate recreation impacts of fire events. In: Tierney, P.T.; Chavez, D.J., tech. coords. Proceedings of the 4th social aspects and recreation research symposium. San Francisco: San Francisco State University: 120–125.

**Englin, J.; Holmes, T.; Lutz, J. [In press].** Wildfires and the economic value of wilderness recreation. In: Holmes, T.; Prestemon, J.; Abt, K., eds. The economics of forest disturbances: wildfires, storms, and pests. Forestry Sciences. Dordrecht, The Netherlands: Springer. Vol. 79.

**Englin, J.; Loomis, J.; González-Cabán, A. 2001.** The dynamic path of recreational values following a forest fire: a comparative analysis of states in the intermountain West. Canadian Journal of Forest Research. 31(10): 1837–1844.

**Gunderson, K.; Watson, A. 2006.** Understanding place meanings on the Bitterroot National Forest–a landscape-level assessment of personal and community values. International Journal of Wilderness. 12(1): 27–31. http://leopold.wilderness.net/pubs/593.pdf. (May 2007).

**Hendricks, W.; Chavez, D.; Phippen, K. 2003.** Observance-influence of fire management and place attachment at Big Sur. In: Jakes, P., comp. Homeowners, communities, and wildfire: science findings from the National Fire Plan: proceedings of the 9th international symposium on society and resource management. Gen. Tech. Rep. NC-231. St. Paul, MN: U.S. Department of Agriculture, Forest Service, North Central Research Station: 45–54.

**Hesseln, H.; Loomis, J.B.; González-Cabán, A. 2004.** The effects of fire on recreation demand in Montana. Western Journal of Applied Forestry. 19(1): 47–53.

**Hesseln, H.; Loomis, J.B.; González-Cabán, A.; Alexander, S. 2003.** Wildfire effects on hiking and biking demand in New Mexico: a travel cost study. Journal of Environmental Management. 69: 359–368.

**Kneeshaw, K.; Vaske, J.J.; Bright, A.D.; Absher, J.D. 2004a.** Acceptability norms toward fire management in three national forests. Environment and Behavior. 36(4): 592–612.

**Kneeshaw, K.; Vaske, J.J.; Bright, A.D.; Absher, J.D. 2004b.** Situational influences of acceptable wildfire management actions. Society and Natural Resources. 17(6): 477–489.

**Knotek, K. 2006.** Trends in public attitudes towards the use of wildland fire. In: Decker, D.; Lardner, M., comps. Proceedings of the 3rd international fire ecology and management congress. Pullman, WA: Washington State University. http://leopold.wilderness.net/pubs/591.pdf. (May 2007).

**Loomis, J.; González-Cabán, A.; Englin, J. 2001.** Testing for differential effects of forest fires on hiking and mountain biking demand and benefits. Journal of Agricultural and Resource Economics. 26(2): 508–522.

**Thapa, B.; Holland, S.; Absher, J. 2004.** The relationship between wildfires and tourist behaviors in Florida: an exploratory study. In: Tierney, P.T.; Chavez, D.J., tech. coord. Proceedings of the 4th social aspects and recreation research symposium. San Francisco: San Francisco State University: 154–161.

**Winter, P.L. 2006.** Urban proximate wilderness visitors' preferences for fire management. In: Decker, D.; Lardner, M., comps. Proceedings of the 3rd international fire ecology and management congress. Pullman, WA: Washington State University. www.emmps.wsu.edu/2006firecongressproceedings/Changes/PatWinter.pdf. (May 25, 2007).

**Winter, P.L.; Cvetkovich, G.T. 2003**. A study of southwesterners' opinions on the management of wildland and wilderness fires: fire management version. http://www.wildfirelessons.net/documents/SDSU_tech_02_FMO eversion.pdf. (May 25, 2007).

**Winter, P.L.; Cvetkovich, G.T. [In press].** An exploration of diversity in southwesterners' views of Forest Service fire management. In: Martin, W.E.; Raish, C.; Kent, B., eds. Wildfire risk: human perceptions and management implications. Washington, DC: Resources for the Future. Chapter 10.

# Assess Economic and Social Costs of Wildland Fire

## Highlight Contact

Jeff Prestemon, Southern Research Station: jprestemon@fs.fed.us

## Relation to Strategic Plan

This work supports the objectives in Portfolio C, Element C2: Socioeconomic aspects of fire and fuels management.

# Background

Wildland fires and society are intricately intertwined. Wildland fires affect goods and services that people value, humans are attracted to features of landscapes that are correlated with wildland fire activity, and humans actively and inadvertently ignite fires and create conditions that exacerbate the impacts of fires. Wildland fires also produce impacts that go far beyond their immediate locations or sectors associated with wildland. Most studies quantifying wildland fire impacts have been limited to timber and property. But the smoke and flames from large wildland fires create immediate human health and safety risks that compel evacuations of entire communities, leading to effects on productive activities in many economic sectors. Such fires can damage such large quantities of timber that their impacts are felt great distances from the impact zone and over many years subsequent to the fire. Fires may not only cause extensive damage to private property but also lead to structural shifts in housing markets to account for altered risk perceptions. Humans play active roles in affecting the risks of wildland fire. First, because people are attracted to wildlands and forests, they build their houses in areas prone to wildland fires, making fires on nearby wildlands potentially more damaging and costly to suppress. Second, people start fires intentionally or accidentally in the course of regular economic activity and pursuing recreational opportunities. Third, people and wildland managers take actions to alter societal risks from wildland fire. Making the best investments in efforts to reduce the overall costs and losses associated with wildland fires requires understanding the full picture of human involvement. Research conducted by Forest Service Research and Development scientists has led to greater understanding of how wildland fires affect society, how society affects wildland fire, and how managerial and other actions can lead to reductions in wildland fire's negative impacts.

**The economic costs of human health and safety risks are often understated.**

## Approach

Research has focused on quantifying the economic effects of wildland fire and understanding the factors influencing the rates of human-caused wildland fires, nationwide. Two large-scale studies have quantified wildland fire impacts in long-run and multisectoral dimensions. (1) A study of the catastrophic wildland fires that occurred in 1998 in Florida (Butry et al. 2001, Mercer et al. 2000) quantified effects on (a) timber damages in terms of economic welfare, including the effects on owners of damaged timber and on consumers and owners of undamaged timber in the region; (b) housing; (c) the health of surrounding populations related to smoke-induced respiratory problems; (d) the hotel and tourism sector owing to required evacuations and other disruptions to economic activity; and (e) suppression expenditures. Although the analysis did not attempt to measure nonmarket or other nontimber damages, it was the first study of its kind to more fully catalogue the spatial and temporal scope of impacts of a large, catastrophic wildland fire on society and the economy. (2) A study of the 2002 Hayman Fire, near Denver, quantified the impacts of the wildland fire on (a) wildland fire suppression, (b) site rehabilitation and restoration, (c) housing, (d) loss of power transmission lines, (e) water storage capacity in an affected reservoir, (f) timber, (g) tourism and recreation, and (h) incidental costs associated with evacuations and public safety. Other costs recognized but not directly quantified included those associated with the regional economy owing to evacuations. Additional analyses evaluated homeowner risk perceptions, protection options, and constraints to self-protection in the event of a wildland fire. Other studies in the area of wildland fire impact assessment include those by Loomis and González-Cabán (1997), which assessed the impact of wildland fire on spotted owl habitat in California and Oregon; Loomis et al. (2002), which assessed impacts in the context of big game habitat; and Loomis et al. (2005), which quantified wildland fire impacts in California, Montana, and Florida in terms of property owner willingness to pay for wildland fire protection. The impacts of wildland fire have also been quantified in terms of housing value and the risk of wildland fire. Notable among these is a study by Stockmann (2006), which evaluated how landscape vegetation and housing features affect the loss probability in the event of wildland fires.

A second pair of studies was more narrowly focused on the timber-sector impacts of wildland fire. Different from previous analyses except for Butry et al. (2001), these studies were able to quantify the short- and long-run welfare effects of two catastrophic western wildland fires: the Bitterroot Fire in Montana in 2001 and the Biscuit Fire in Oregon in 2002. The Bitterroot study evaluated the timber-related welfare losses experienced by producers and consumers. A major contribution of that analysis was in quantifying, in timber welfare terms, the economic impacts of the planning and litigation-related delays in the initiation of timber salvage in the aftermath of the event (Prestemon et al. 2006.) The Biscuit Fire analysis also quantified the effects of hypothetical delays. The contribution of that analysis was that it applied a spatial equilibrium modeling technique to quantify the decline with distance in the price and welfare impacts of the wildland fire and the salvage (Prestemon and Holmes, in press).

Two studies compose a third area of analysis, focusing on quantifying the effects of fire risk on property values. The first study evaluated the effects of a catastrophic wildland fire on housing values in Washington state (Huggett 2003; Huggett et al., in press). An important contribution of this work was that it captured the short- and long-run housing price effects of the wildland fire, the first known study of its kind. The second (Donovan et al. 2007) evaluated how a newly implemented community fire-risk rating system for individual properties implemented in Colorado Springs, Colorado, resulted in changes in housing values. A primary finding was that house construction materials have a large, significant effect on housing values that have information.

The fourth area of research focused on human-caused fire. There are two main lines of analysis. One evaluates the underlying drivers of wildland arson and its spatiotemporal patterns. The other evaluates the factors most important to all kinds of human-caused fires. Models of wildland arson have, for the first time, quantified the daily clustering patterns of arson wildland fires at the scale of small counties, identified the linkage between wildland arson and economic conditions, demonstrated the role of law enforcement in reducing the number of arson ignitions, characterized the role of fuels management in reducing the damages from wildland arson, and placed the arson ignition process in the context of an economic model of crime (Prestemon and Butry 2005; Prestemon and Butry, in press a, in press b[3]). These findings largely have been confirmed for arson on California national forests, as well (Prestemon and Butry, in press b). Other Florida-focused research has measured the differences in the rates of spatiotemporal clustering of fires among lightning and several categories of individual anthropogenic fire causes

---

[3] Butry, D.T.; Prestemon, J.P. 2005. Spatio-temporal wildland arson crime functions. Paper presented at the annual meeting of the American Agricultural Economics Association. 18 p. Unpublished paper. On file with: Jeffrey P. Prestemon, Forestry Sciences Laboratory, P.O. Box 12254, Research Triangle Park, NC 27709.

(Genton et al. 2006), quantified the role of climate and weather on human-caused wildland fires of different categories, identified the annual autoregressive nature of human-caused wildland fires, measured the effects of various fuels management efforts on the rates of human-caused wildland fires across broad landscapes (Butry 2006, Mercer and Prestemon 2005, Prestemon et al. 2002), and quantified how human-caused fires are set closer to valuable property than lightning fires (Butry et al. 2002), and measured how human-caused wildland fires may be related to managerial activities (Prestemon et al. 2002, Pye et al. 2003). Ongoing research seeks to connect large-scale and long-term crime patterns to wildland arson, develop crime hotspotting models for use by law enforcement, and understand how education and public awareness campaigns may affect the rates of human-caused wildland fires. The latter study is underway and is focused on the efficacy of prevention programs in Florida and on national forests of the United States.

## Products and Tools

Many of the most recent advances in our understanding of the economic impacts of wildland fire, human-caused fires, and the efficacy of wildland fire interventions are captured in a soon-to-be-released book. This volume *The Economics of Forest Disturbances: Wildfires, Storms, and Invasive Species* (Holmes et al., in press) has 19 chapters covering topics ranging from describing the production of all types of wildland fires and other forest disturbances; quantifying the impacts of these disturbances on timber, private property, and government expenditures; characterizing how interventions into wildland fire and other disturbance processes can lead to net societal gains; and characterizing the economics of societal and managerial incentives to manage landscapes and suppress disturbances.

## Results and Application

Results of the studies examining the impacts of the Bitterroot and Biscuit Fires made up part of the salvage environmental impact statements for these in the Northern Region (Region 1) and Pacific Southwest Region (Region 5), respectively.

## Awards and Recognitions

The Biscuit Fire analysis applied research approaches and contributed to a timber salvage environmental impact statement (Prestemon et al. 2003) and continues to inform debate about government timber salvage decisions following the wildland fire. The technical advances in salvage economics research provided a foundation for a policy analysis recently requested by the Congressional Budget Office.

## Principal Investigators

David T. Butry, david.butry@nist.gov: National Institute of Standards and Technology; Thomas P. Holmes, tholmes@fs.fed.us; Robert Huggett, Jr., rhuggett@fs.fed.us: Southern Research Station; Krista Gebert, kgebert@fs.fed.us: Rocky Mountain Research Station; Armando González-Cabán, agonzalezcaban@fs.fed.us: Pacific Southwest Research Station; Gregory Jones gjones@fs.fed.us; Brian Kent, bkent@fs.fed.us: Rocky Mountain Research Station; Evan Mercer, emercer@fs.fed.us; Jeffrey P. Prestemon, jprestemon@fs.fed.us; John M. Pye, jpye@fs.fed.us: Southern Research Station

## Key Partners

National Institute of Standards and Technology; University of Montana; Forest Service, National Forest System, State and Private Forestry; Colorado State University; North Carolina State University; Texas Tech University

## Funding

This research was supported by the Joint Fire Science Program and the National Fire Plan; Forest Service Research and Development, and State and Private Forestry.

## Literature Cited

**Butry, D.T. 2006**. Estimating the efficacy of wildfire management using propensity scores. Raleigh, NC: North Carolina State University. 110 p. Ph.D. dissertation.

**Butry, D.T.; Mercer, D.E.; Prestemon, J.P.; Pye, J.M.; Holmes, T.P. 2001**. What is the price of catastrophic wildfire? Journal of Forestry. 99(11): 9–17.

**Butry, D.T.; Pye, J.M.; Prestemon, J.P. 2002**. Prescribed fire in the interface: separating the people from the trees. In: Outcalt, K.W., ed. Proceedings of the 11th biennial Southern silvicultural research conference. Gen. Tech. Rep. SRS–48. Asheville, NC: U.S. Department of Agriculture, Forest Service, Southern Research Station: 132–136.

**Donovan, G.H.; Champ, P.A.; Butry, D.T. 2007.** The impact of wildfire risk on housing price: a case study from Colorado Springs. Land Economics. 83(2): 217–233.

**Genton, M.G.; Butry, D.T.; Gumpertz, M.; Prestemon, J.P. 2006.** Spatio-temporal analysis of wildfire ignitions in the St. Johns River water management district. International Journal of Wildland Fire. 15: 87–97.

**Holmes, T.P.; Prestemon, J.P.; Abt, K.L., eds. [In press].** The economics of forest disturbances: wildfires, storms, and invasive species. Forestry Sciences. Dordrecht, The Netherlands: Springer. Vol 79.

**Huggett, R.J. 2003.** Fire in the wildland-urban interface: an examination of the effects of wildfire on residential property markets. Raleigh, NC: North Carolina State University. 136 p. Ph.D. dissertation. http://www.lib.ncsu.edu/theses/available/etd-07302003-165922/unrestricted/etd.pdf. (May 2007).

**Huggett, R.J., Jr.; Murphy, E.A.; Holmes, T.P. [In press].** Forest disturbance impacts on residential property values. In: Holmes, T.P.; Prestemon, J.P.; Abt, K.L., eds. The economics of forest disturbances: wildfires, storms, and invasive species. Forestry Sciences. Dordrecht, The Netherlands: Springer. Vol 79.

**Loomis, J.B.; González-Cabán, A. 1997.** Comparing the economic value of reducing fire risk to spotted owl habitat in California and Oregon. Forest Science. 43(4): 473–482.

**Loomis, J.B.; Griffith, D.; Wu, E.; González-Cabán, A. 2002.** Estimating the economic value of big game habitat production from prescribed fire using a time series approach. Journal of Forest Economics. 8(2): 119–129.

**Loomis, J.B.; Le, H.T.; González-Cabán, A. 2005.** Testing transferability of willingness to pay for forest fire prevention among three states of California, Florida, and Montana. Journal of Forest Economics. 11(3): 125–140.

**Mercer, D.E.; Prestemon, J.P. 2005.** Comparing production function models for wildfire risk analysis in the wildland-urban interface. Forest Policy and Economics. 7(5): 782–795.

**Mercer, D.E.; Pye, J.M.; Prestemon, J.P.; Butry, D.T.; Holmes, T.P. 2000.** Economic effects of catastrophic wildfires: assessing the effectiveness of fuel reduction programs for reducing the economic impacts of catastrophic forest fire events. Final report. Topic 8 of the Research Grant Economic and Ecological Consequences of the 1998 Florida Wildfires. http://www.fl-dof.com/publications/joint_fire_sciences/jfs_pdf/economic_effects.pdf). On file with: D. Evan Mercer, Forestry Sciences Laboratory, P.O. Box 12254, Research Triangle Park, NC 27709.

**Prestemon, J.P.; Butry, D.T. 2005.** Time to burn: modeling wildland arson as an autoregressive crime function. American Journal of Agricultural Economics. 87(3): 756–770.

**Prestemon, J.P.; Butry, D.T. [In press a].** Wildland arson: a research assessment. In: Beatty, J.J.; Lee, D.C.; Pye, J.M.; Sands, Y., eds. Proceedings on advances in threat assessment and their application to forest and rangeland management conference. Gen. Tech. Rep. Asheville, NC: U.S. Department of Agriculture, Forest Service, Southern Research Station. http://forestencyclopedia.net. (May 9, 2007).

**Prestemon, J.P.; Butry, D.T. [In press b].** Wildland arson management. In: Holmes, T.P.; Prestemon, J.P.; Abt, K.L., eds. The economics of forest disturbances: wildfires, storms, and invasive species. Forestry Sciences. Dordrecht, The Netherlands: Springer. Vol 79.

**Prestemon, J.P.; Holmes, T.P. [In press].** Timber salvage economics. In: Holmes, T.P.; Prestemon, J.P.; Abt, K.L., eds. The economics of forest disturbances: wildfires, storms, and invasive species. Forestry Sciences. Dordrecht, The Netherlands: Springer. Vol 79.

**Prestemon, J.P.; Pye, J.M.; Butry, D.T.; Holmes, T.P.; Mercer, D.E. 2002.** Understanding broad scale wildfire risks in a human-dominated landscape. Forest Science. 48(4): 685–693.

**Prestemon, J.P.; Wear, D.N.; Holmes, T.P. 2003.** Biscuit Fire salvage impacts analysis. Report prepared for the Pacific Northwest Region (Region 6). On file with: Jeffrey P. Prestemon, Forestry Sciences Laboratory, P.O. Box 12254, Research Triangle Park, NC 27709.

**Prestemon, J.P.; Wear, D.N.; Holmes, T.P.; Stewart, F. 2006.** Wildfire, timber salvage, and the economics of expediency. Forest Policy and Economics. 8(3): 312–322.

**Pye, J.M.; Prestemon, J.P.; Butry, D.T.; Abt, K.L. 2003**. Prescribed burning and wildfire risk in the 1998 fire season in Florida. In: Omi, P., ed. Conference on fire, fuel treatments and ecological restoration. Gen. Tech. Rep. RMRS-P-29. Fort Collins, CO: U.S. Department of Agriculture, Forest Service, Rocky Mountain Research Station: 15–26.

**Stockmann, K. 2006**. A cost effectiveness analysis of preventative mitigation options for wildland urban interface homes threatened by wildfire. Missoula, MT: University of Montana. 185 p. Ph.D. dissertation.

## Additional Reading

**Kent, B.; Gebert, K.; McCaffrey, S.; Martin, W.; Calkin, D.; Schuster, E.; Martin, I.; Bender, H.W.; Alward, G.; Kumagai, Y.; Cohn, P.J.; Carroll, M.; Williams, D.; Ekarius, C. 2003**. Social and economic issues of the Hayman Fire. In: Graham, R.T., ed. Hayman Fire case study. Gen. Tech. Rep. RMRS-GTR-114 (Revision). Fort Collins, CO: U.S. Department of Agriculture, Forest Service, Rocky Mountain Research Station: 315–396.

# Community Wildland Fire Preparedness

## Highlight Contact

Pamela Jakes, Northern Research Station: pjakes@fs.fed.us

## Relation to Strategic Plan

The work reported here is primarily related to Portfolio C, Element C1: Public interactions with fire and fuels management.

# Background

In recent years, a number of programs and initiatives have been implemented to help communities prepare for wildland fires and manage hazardous fuels. The National Fire Plan [NFP] has provided financial support for community-level wildland fire preparedness, and a number of programs provide technical assistance. This research identifies lessons learned from a number of communities that provide direction to other communities seeking to improve wildland fire preparedness.

# Approach

Case studies were conducted in states representing a range of biological, physical, and social contexts. Researchers employed key informant interviews, focus groups,

P.J. Jakes

Widening driveways to improve access for emergency vehicles and numbering properties to speed up identification are just two ways property owners and communities can improve their wildland fire preparedness.

surveys, and attendance at community gatherings to collect qualitative and quantitative data that document community actions and programs to improve wildland fire preparedness, build community capacity, and sustain these efforts long term.

## Products and Tools

A set of case study summaries on community wildland fire preparedness highlights what communities can accomplish in reducing wildland fire risk. View the Community Responses to Wildland Fire Threats Web site (http://www.ncsu.edu/ project/ wildfire) and the Northern Research Station's Wildland Fire-Community Fire Preparedness Case Studies Web site (http://www.ncrs.fs.fed.us/4803/focus/fire/ community_preparedness/cp_case_studies/). A Web-based tool was developed that serves as a learning community for those engaged with the public in collaboratively developing community wildland fire protection plans (http://jfsp.fortlewis.edu/). The user-friendly, searchable National Database of State and Local Wildfire Hazard Mitigation Programs Web site (http://www.wildfireprograms.usda.gov) describes 232 states and local wildland fire mitigation programs across 37 states, including community actions such as wildland fire protection planning, educational programs, defensible space regulations, and fuel reduction incentives for property owners. This site serves as a clearinghouse of ideas for fire protection officials, natural resource professionals, and community leaders. As part of the Living With Fire in Chaparral Ecosystems Working Group on people and ecosystem interface, a summit for managers, community leaders, and researchers served as a forum for sharing the

**There are practical ways communities can increase preparedness.**

P.J. Jakes

Case studies help researchers to answer the "how" and "why" questions.

P.J. Jakes

Programs like Firewise Communities/USA help communities build physical preparedness.

latest approaches to fire management for communities, and key findings on communication with communities before, during, and after a fire event.

## Results and Applications

As a result of this research, communities across the country are taking action to improve physical preparedness (for example, vegetation management, new or improved communication systems, and public education programs) and social preparedness (for example, planning and training; Fege and Absher, in press; Jakes et al. 2007; Steelman and Kunkel 2004; Steelman et al. 2004). A number of partners have played varied roles in community preparedness, working collaboratively to achieve local and national goals (Jakes et al. 2004). Additionally, residents in fire-prone communities recognize the responsibility they and fellow community members have in reducing risk (Winter and Cvetkovich, in press). Communities that succeed in building preparedness need a strong foundation, often referred to as community capacity (Jakes et al. 2007).

Research findings have also helped direct and generate support for wildland-fire preparedness activities in communities across the country. Community fire organizations such as Firewise Communities committees and Fire Safe Councils are using findings in their communication, education, and preparedness efforts. Professional organizations, such as the National Academy of Public Administration, the

American Planning Association, and the American Society of Landscape Architects, have also found the summaries useful for training and educating members who can be major players in wildland-fire preparedness.

## Principal Investigators

James Absher, jabsher@fs.fed.us; Deborah Chavez, dchavez@fs.fed.us: Pacific Southwest Station; Terry Haines, thaines01@fs.fed.us: Southern Research Station; Pamela Jakes, pjakes@fs.fed.us: Northern Research Station; Linda Kruger, lkruger@fs.fed.us: Pacific Northwest Research Station; Evan Mercer, emercer@fs.fed.us: Southern Research Station; Daniel Williams, drwilliams@fs.fed.us: Rocky Mountain Research Station; Patricia Winter, pwinter@fs.fed.us: Pacific Southwest Research Station

## Key Partners

Bureau of Land Management, Colorado State University, Fort Lewis College, Inland Empire Fire Safe Council Alliance, Louisiana State University, North Carolina State University, San Diego Natural History Museum, San Diego Fire Recovery Network, Southern Oregon University, Texas A&M, Washington State University, Western Washington University, University of Minnesota, University of Florida, U.S. Geological Survey

## Funding

National Fire Plan, Joint Fire Science Program

## Literature Cited

**Fege, A.; Absher J.D. [In press]**. Inviting other professions to help reduce wildfire property losses. Fire Management Today.

**Jakes, P.J.; Kruger, L.; Monroe, M.; Nelson, K.; Sturtevant, V. 2004**. Partners in wildland fire preparedness: lessons from communities in the US. Conference proceedings: 3rd international symposium on human behavior in fire: public fire safety, professionals in partnership. London: Interscience Communications Ltd: 139–150.

**Jakes, P.J.; Kruger, L.; Monroe, M.; Nelson, K.; Sturtevant, V. 2007**. Improving wildfire preparedness: lessons from communities across the US. Human Ecology Review. 14(2): 182–191.

**Steelman, T.A.; Kunkel, G.F. 2004**. Effective community responses to wild-fire threats: lessons from New Mexico. Society and Natural Resources. 17(8): 679–700.

**Steelman, T.A.; Kunkel, G.F.; Bell, D. 2004**. Federal and state influence on community responses to wildfire in Arizona, Colorado and New Mexico. Journal of Forestry. 102(6): 21–27.

**Winter, P.L.; Cvetkovich, G.T. [In press]** Perceptions, impact, actions, shared values and trust: the experience of community residents in a fire-prone ecosystem. In: Beatty, J.J.; Lee, D.C.; Pye, J.M.; Sands, Y., eds. Proceedings on advances in threat assessment and their application to forest and rangeland management conference. Gen. Tech. Rep. Asheville, NC: U.S. Department of Agriculture, Forest Service, Southern Research Station. http://forestencyclopedia.net. (May 9, 2007).

## Additional Readings

**Haines, T.K.; Renner, C.R.; Reams, M.A. 2005.** Mitigating wildfire risk in the wildland urban interface: the role of regulations. In: Aguirre-Bravo, C.; Pellicane, P.J.; Burns, D.P.; Draggan, S., eds. Monitoring science and technology symposium: unifying knowledge for sustainability in the Western Hemisphere proceedings. Proceedings RMRS-P-42CD. Fort Collins, CO: U.S. Department of Agriculture, Forest Service, Rocky Mountain Research Station: 715–722.

**Haines, T.K.; Renner, C.R.; Reams, M.A. [In press].** Reducing wildfire risk in the wildland-urban interface: regulation of land-use and vegetation management practives. In: Holmes, T.P.; Prestemon, J.P.; Abt, K.L., eds. The economics of forest disturbances: wildfires, storms, and invasive species. Foresty Sciences. Dordrecht, The Netherlands: Springer. Vol. 79.

**Haines, T.K.; Renner, C.R.; Reams, M.A.; Granskog, J.E. 2004**. The national wildfire mitigation program database: state, county, and local efforts to reduce wildfire risk. In: Proceedings of the Society of American Foresters national convention: one forest under two flags. Bethesda, MD: Society of American Foresters. 31(4): 357.

**Jakes, P.J., comp. 2004.** Homeowners, communities, and wildfire; science findings from the National Fire Plan: proceedings of the 9th international symposium on society and resource management. Gen. Tech. Rep. NC-231. St. Paul, MN: U.S. Department of Agriculture, Forest Service, North Central Research Station. 92 p.

**Jakes, P.J.; Nelson, K. 2007.** Community interaction with large wildland fire events: critical initiatives prior to the fire. In: Daniel, T.C.; Carroll, M.S.; Moseley, C.; Raish, C., eds. People, fire, and forests: a synthesis of wildfire social science. Corvallis, OR: Oregon State University Press: 91–103.

**Olson, C.; Shindler, B. 2007.** Citizen-agency interactions in planning and decisionmaking after large fires. Gen. Tech. Rep. PNW-GTR-715. Portland, OR: U.S. Department of Agriculture, Forest Service, Pacific Northwest Research Station. 38 p.

**Reams, M.A.; Haines, T.K.; Renner, C.R.; Wascom, M.; Kingre, H. 2005.** Goals, obstacles, and effective strategies of wildfire mitigation programs in the wildland-urban interface. Forest Policy and Economics. 7(5): 818–826.

**Taylor, J.G.; Gillette, S.C.; Hodgson, R.W.; Downing, J.L. 2005.** Communicating with wildland interface communities during wildfire. Open-file report 2005–1061. 26 p. Reston, VA: U.S. Department of the Interior, Geological Survey. www.fort.usgs.gov/products/publications/21455/21455.asp. (April 2007).

**Vogt, C.A. 2004.** Consideration of property risk reduction at the time of home purchase by wildland-urban interface (WUI) homeowners. In: Murdy, J.J., comp., ed. Proceedings of the 2003 Northeastern recreation research symposium. Gen. Tech. Rep. NE-317. Newtown Square, PA: U.S. Department of Agriculture, Forest Service, Northeastern Research Station: 11–17.

# Evaluate Opportunities for Biomass Processing Facility Siting and Economic Feasibility of Landscape-Scale Fuel Treatment

## Highlight Contacts

Jeremy Fried: jeremy.fried@fs.fed.us; Jamie Barbour: jbarbour01@fs.fed.us; Pacific Northwest Research Station

## Relation to Strategic Plan

The work reported here is primarily related to Portfolio D: Integrated fire and fuels management research; Element D3: Biomass utilization, product development and forest operations associated with fire and fuel management activities. Also Portfolio E: Develop and deliver knowledge and tools; Element E1: Synthesis and tool development.

## Background

Landscape-scale deployment of mechanical thinning of western forests to reduce fuel accumulations, as called for by the Healthy Forests Restoration Act, has been slow to materialize, in large part owing to the limited availability of funds to subsidize such activities, the high costs of these labor-intensive treatments, and the low to nonexistent commercial value of the majority of the trees removed in such operations. Construction of facilities that would convert biomass to energy is seen as a prospect for generating new markets for small-diameter wood, and potentially contributing to expansion of the scope of fuel treatment possibilities. Answering the questions of where to construct such facilities, and the appropriate scale at which to do so, depends, among other things, on the location and quantity of the resources upon which they will draw and the costs of transporting harvested material across the landscape. Biomass plant investors and operators, fuels managers, state and private foresters, and community planners are keenly interested in answers to such questions.

**The financial barriers to large-scale fuel treatments vary across the west.**

## Approach

The Forest Inventory and Analysis (FIA) BioSum analysis framework was developed to combine forest inventory data representing an analysis region, a treatment cost model, a fuel treatment effectiveness model, and a raw material hauling cost model to explore alternative landscape-scale treatment scenarios that achieve a variety of management objectives (Fried 2003, Fried et al. 2005). Raw material volumes generated by mechanical fire-hazard-reduction treatments are estimated by applying silvicultural treatments to data derived from forest inventory plots; estimates of treatment costs are generated via the Fuel Reduction Cost Simulator (Fight et al. 2006); gross product values are calculated as the product of modeled harvest quantities and local product prices; and a variety of treatments, developed in consultations with local silviculturists and fire management experts, are simulated to assess treatment effectiveness and net and gross treatment costs (Fried and Christensen 2004, Fried et al. 2003). Candidate sites for building processing facilities can be simulated and evaluated with respect to economic feasibility (Fried et al. 2005), or the framework can be extended via mixed-integer optimization to jointly select treatments for each acre and site-suitable expansion of processing capacity (Daugherty and Fried 2007).

## Products and Tools

The FIA BioSum model has been applied to a 25-million-acre region of Oregon and California and to the entirety of Arizona and New Mexico in support of research studies and articles (e.g., Barbour et al., in press; Bilek et al. 2005), presentations to Washington office, regional and forest staffs, other scientists, forest and fire managers, and the biomass-to-energy community. The FIA BioSum simulation software, which provides users with a user-friendly, automated, integrated analysis environment and all the needed model components to conduct BioSum analyses for any area in the United States for which FIA plot and road network data are available, is in beta release, and documentation, an on-line help subsystem, sample data sets, and a user tutorial are nearing completion.

## Results and Applications

Under a range of policy scenarios with different objectives in the Oregon and California regional analysis, removal of considerable amounts of commercial-size trees is needed to accomplish fire hazard reduction goals when objectives are centered on either maximizing net revenue or maximizing treatment effectiveness. Even if the objective is to minimize merchantable volume, about two-thirds of the removed weight would be in saw logs. Tops and limbs from merchantable commercial conifers and whole trees of hardwoods and noncommercial conifers are major sources of submerchantable wood for which there is essentially no market but bioenergy. Assuming a 10-year implementation and depreciation of the biomass plants constructed to support fuel treatment, and treatment of all acres for which treatments would achieve fuel reduction benefits, the study region is capable of annually producing $590 million in net revenue, yielding 6 to 12 million green tons of biomass and 840 million to 1.2 billion cubic feet of merchantable wood, and over the course of a decade, achieving effective treatment of 2.8 to 8.1 million acres while providing bioenergy capacity of 496 to 1009 megawatts (MW). Analysis with a range of forest bioenergy-facility capacities revealed robustness in the optimal spatial distribution of bioenergy facilities. This robustness depends on the extent of the transportation network relative to the sources of woody biomass and on the ability to change plot-treatment combinations to define different biomass collection areas. Custom analyses have been conducted in support of biomass plant capacity decisions (in Lakeview, Oregon), forest practices policy development (by the California Department of Forestry and Fire in California), and regional analysis of opportunities to attract bioenergy investment capital (in New Mexico).

## Awards and Recognition

Director's award for FIA excellence for fiscal year (FY) 2002, USDA Forest Service. For outstanding research in the development and implementation of the BioSum model to assess the economic and fire risk impacts of treating stands across broad landscapes.

INFORMS 2004 Best paper (out of 25) in forestry sponsored sessions award, Institute for Management Science and Operations Research, Section on Energy, Natural Resources and the Environment. Presentation by J.S. Fried and P.J. Daugherty, *Joint optimization of fuel treatment selection and processing facility siting for landscape-scale fire hazard reduction.*

## Principal Investigators

Jeremy Fried, jeremy.fried@fs.fed.us; Jamie Barbour, jbarbour01@fs.fed.us; Roger Fight (now retired) Pacific Northwest Research Station

## Funding

National Fire Plan; Pacific Northwest Research Station, Forest Inventory and Analysis Program; Western Forest Leadership Coalition

# Literature Cited

**Barbour, R.J.; Fried, J.S.; Daugherty, P.J.; Fight, R. [In press].** Predicting the potential mix of wood products available from timbershed scale fire hazard reduction treatments. Forest Policy and Economics.

**Bilek, E.M.; Skog, K.E.; Fried, J.S.; Christensen, G. 2005.** Fuel to burn: economics of converting forest thinnings to energy using BioMax in southern Oregon. Gen. Tech. Rep. FPL-GTR-157. Madison, WI: U.S. Department of Agriculture, Forest Service, Forest Products Laboratory. 27 p.

**Daugherty, P.J.; Fried, J.S. 2007.** Jointly optimizing selection of fuel treatments and siting of forest biomass-based energy production facilities for landscape-scale fire hazard reduction. INFOR: Information Systems and Operational Research. 45(1).

**Fight, R.D.; Hartsough, B.R.; Noordijk, P. 2006.** Users guide for FRCS: fuel reduction cost simulator software. Gen. Tech. Rep. PNW-GTR-668. Portland, OR: U.S. Department of Agriculture, Forest Service, Pacific Northwest Research Station. 23 p.

**Fried, J.S. 2003.** Evaluating landscape-scale fuel treatment policies with FIA data. Western Forester. 48(1): 6–7.

**Fried, J.S.; Barbour, R.J.; Fight, R. 2003.** FIA BioSum: applying a multi-scale evaluation tool in southwest Oregon. Journal of Forestry. 101(2): 8.

**Fried, J.S.; Christensen, G. 2004.** FIA BioSum: a tool to evaluate financial costs, opportunities, and effectiveness of fuel treatments. Western Forester. 49(5): 12–13.

**Fried, J.S.; Christensen, G.; Weyermann, D.; Barbour, R.J.; Fight, R.; Hiserote, B.; Pinjuv, G. 2005.** Modeling opportunities and feasibility of siting wood-fired electrical generating facilities to facilitate landscape-scale fuel treatment with FIA BioSum. In: Bevers, M.; Barrett, T.M., comps. Systems analysis in forest resources: proceedings of the 2003 symposium. Gen. Tech. Rep. PNW-GTR-656. Portland, OR: U.S. Department of Agriculture, Forest Service, Pacific Northwest Research Station: 195–204.

# Human Factors in Fire Management

## Highlight Contact

Armando González-Cabán, Pacific Southwest Research Station:
agonzalezcaban@fs.fed.us

## Relation to Strategic Plan

This work supports objectives in Portfolio C, Element C3: Organizational
effectiveness.

# Background

Although most wildland fires are suppressed effectively in initial or extended
attack, occasionally fires become exceptionally large, resulting in unusual resource
damages, significant financial impacts, and possibly loss of life. Understanding how
to better manage fires (where it is desired and undesired), and to improve methods
for controlling their costs and impacts requires a detailed knowledge of the
decisionmaking processes that were ongoing prior to and during the incident.

# Approach

Decision and risk science approaches as well as organizational and individual
behavior theory and the policy sciences have been used to understand large fires—
including costs, wildland fire use, and prescribed fire planning and operations, high
reliability, safety, and sense-making on the fire-line. To understand managers'
decision space, researchers developed a model for decomposing and reconstructing
large-fire decision processes, including influence diagrams, decision tree analysis,
multiattribute utility analysis (MAU), and other models based on decision process
tracing methodologies. To understand the factors influencing large-fire suppression
costs, a survey of members of national incident management teams (IMT) determine how their structure, functions, and decision space potentially affect suppression costs.

# Products and Tools

The "Event Frame" methodology has been tested in actual fire incidents
(MacGregor and González-Cabán 2004). By identifying crucial decision events
at different stages of the incidents and the factors that affect them, fire managers
can possibly identify areas for suppression costs savings.

The wildland fire situation analysis (WFSA) evaluation led to development of a decision skills curriculum to improve training for fire managers and fire planners (González-Cabán and MacGregor 1998). The paper-based WFSA tool was substantially revised and updated, then fully computerized and placed on the Forest Service Web site for download directly by users.

## Results and Applications

The majority of IMT members feel that although cost containment and effectiveness are in the forefront of their decisionmaking process, the decision space in which they operate leaves them with little room for major cost-reduction decisions (Canton-Thompson et al. 2006). These findings echo those of MacGregor and González-Cabán (2004) and support the need for further basic research in this area. Research into how institutional and managerial constraints affect prescribed burning costs found that the single most influential factor affecting prescribed burning costs was the individual manager's risk posture (González-Cabán 1997). A national survey of the fire management community uncovered the importance of understanding degree of risk tolerance in how fire management decisions are made (Winter and Bigler-Cole 2006). To help improve incident planning, a survey of incident commanders was undertaken; it showed that lack of training and necessary skills in how to use existing decision-support tools, such as the WFSA leads to improper use.

From 1999 through 2005, 450 federal and state fire personnel have taken the decision skills training course throughout the Forest Service regions. Efforts to bring organizational theory to the fire community has resulted in four national workshops on high-reliability theory ("Managing the Unexpected," approximately 400 attendees since 2004) a national workshop on conducting after-action reviews, establishment of the interagency Wildland Fire Lessons Learned Center, and efforts to understand the causes of prescribed fire escapes (Black and Dether 2006).

## Principal Investigators

Armando González-Cabán, agonzalezcaban@fs.fed.us; Patricia Winter, pwinter@fs.fed.us: Pacific Southwest Research Station; David E. Calkin, dcalkin@fs.fed.us; Janie Canton-Thompson, jcantonthompson@fs.fed.us: Rocky Mountain Research Station; Geoffrey Donovan, gdonovan@fs.fed.us: Pacific Northwest Research Station; Krista Gebert, kgebert@fs.fed.us; Anne Black, aeblack@fs.fed.us; James Saveland, jsaveland@fs.fed.us; Alan Watson, awatson@fs.fed.us: Rocky Mountain Research Station

## Key Partners

MacGregor-Bates, Inc., Decision Research, Rocky Mountain Research Station, University of Michigan, Harvard University, Massachusetts Institute of Technology, National Park Service, Bureau of Land Management, Fish and Wildlife Service, Bureau of Indian Affairs

## Funding

Joint Fire Science Program, National Fire Plan

## Literature Cited

**Black, A.E.; Dether, D. 2006**. Learning from escaped prescribed fires—lessons for high reliability. Fire Management Today. 66(4): 50–56. http://leopold.wilderness.net/staff/black.htm. (May 9, 2007).

**Canton-Thompson, J.; Thompson, B.; Gebert, K.; Calkin, D.; Donovan, G.; Jones, G. 2006**. Factors affecting suppression costs as identified by incident management teams. Res. Note RMSR-RN-30. Fort Collins, CO: U.S. Department of Agriculture, Forest Service, Rocky Mountain Research Station. 12 p. http://www.fs.fed.us/rm/pubs/rmrs_rn030.pdf. (May 9, 2007).

**González-Cabán, A. 1997**. Managerial and institutional factors affect prescribed burning costs. Forest Sciences. 43(4): 535–543. http://www.ingentaconnect.com/content/saf/fs/1997/00000043/00000004/art00011. (May 9, 2007).

**González-Cabán, A.; MacGregor, D.G. 1998**. Improving decision making process for the Forest Service's wildland fire situation analysis. In: Viegas, D.X., ed. Proceedings of the 3rd international conference on forest fire research and 14th conference on fire and forest meteorology. Lisbon, Portugal: University of Coimbra: 2209–2225. Vol. 1, E18. http://www.eufirelab.org/toolbox2/library/references.php?pageNum_References=20&totalRows_References=2031. (May 9, 2007).

**MacGregor, D.; González-Cabán, A. 2004**. Framework for representing large-fire decisions and outcomes. In: González-Cabán, A., ed. Proceedings of the 2nd symposium on fire economics, planning and policy: a global view [CD-ROM]. On file with: Armando González-Cabán, Forest Fire Laboratory, 4955 Canyon Crest Drive, Riverside, CA 92507. http://www.eu-medin.org/cordoba/fireec04/papers/23.pdf. (May 9, 2007).

**Winter, P.L.; Bigler-Cole, H. 2006**. Improving a national fire information program: a needs assessment approach. Proceedings of the 3rd international fire ecology and management congress. [DVD, track 2, public perception]. www.emmps.wsu.edu/2006firecongressproceedings. (May 9, 2007).

## Additional Readings

**Black, A.M.; Williamson, D.; Doane, D. [In press]**. Wildland fire use barriers and facilitators. Fire Management Today.

**Doane, D.; O'Laughlin, J.; Morgan, P.; Miller, C. 2006**. Barriers to wildland fire use: a preliminary problem analysis. International Journal of Wilderness. 12: 36–38.

**Keller, P., ed. 2004**. Managing the unexpected in prescribed fire use operations: a workshop on the high reliability organization. Gen. Tech. Rep. RMRS-GTR-137. Fort Collins, CO: U.S. Department of Agriculture, Forest Service, Rocky Mountain Research Station. 73 p.

**Knotek, K.; Watson, A.E. 2006**. Organizational characteristics that contribute to success in engaging the public to accomplish fuels management at the wilderness/non-wilderness interface. In: Andrews, P.L.; Butler, B.W., comps. Fuels management—how to measure success: conference proceedings. Proceedings RMRS-P-41. Fort Collins, CO: U.S. Department of Agriculture, Forest Service, Rocky Mountain Research Station: 703–713.

**Laband, D.; González-Cabán, A.; Hussain, A. 2006**. Factors that influence administrative appeals of proposed USDA Forest Service fuels reduction actions. Forest Science. 52(5): 477–488.

**Larson, G.; Wright, V.; Spaulding, C.; Rossetto, K.; Rausch, G.; Richards, A.; Durnford, S. [In press]**. Using social science to understand and improve wildland fire organizations: an annotated list of readings. Gen. Tech. Rep. Fort Collins, CO: U.S. Department of Agriculture, Forest Service, Rocky Mountain Research Station.

**Loomis, J.; Muller, J.; González-Cabán, A.; Champ, J. 2004**. Comparison of survey administration mode in determining public support and willingness to pay for prescribed burning in California. In: González-Cabán, A., ed. Proceedings of the 2nd international symposium on fire economics, planning, and policy: a global view. [CD-ROM]. On file with: Armando González-Cabán, Forest Fire Laboratory, 4955 Canyon Crest Drive, Riverside, CA 92507. http://www.eu medin.org/cordoba/fireec04/papers/23.pdf. (May 9, 2007).

**Loomis, J.B.; Bair, L.S.; González-Cabán, A. 2001**. Prescribed fire and public support: Knowledge gained, attitudes change in Florida. Journal of Forestry. 99(11): 18–23.

**MacGregor, D.; Finucane, M.; González-Cabán, A. [In press]**. Risk perception, adaptation and behavior change: self-protection in the wildland-urban interface. In: Martin, W.E.; Raish, C.; Kent, B., eds. Wildfire risk: human perception and management implications. Washington, DC: Resources for the Future. Chapter 9.

**Thomas, D. [In press]**. Capturing the deep smarts of fire behavior and fuels experts. Proceedings of the 2nd fire behavior and fuels conference. Destin, FL: [Publisher unknown].

**Williamson, M.A. [In press]**. Factors in United States Forest Service district rangers' decision to manage a fire for resource benefit. International Journal of Wildland Fire.

**Winter, P.L.; Bigler-Cole, H. [In press]**. Information needs, tolerance for risk, and protection from risk: the case of national predictive services customers. In: Beatty, J.J.; Lee, D.C.; Pye, J.M.; Sands, Y., eds. Proceedings on advances in threat assessment and their application to forest and rangeland management conference. Asheville, NC: U.S. Department of Agriculture, Forest Service, Southern Research Stations. http//forestencyclopedia.net. (May 9, 2007).

# Optimal Fire and Fuels Management

## Highlight Contacts

Evan Mercer, Southern Research Station: emercer@fs.fed.us; Greg Jones, Rocky Mountain Research Station: jgjones@fs.fed.us

## Relation to Strategic Plan

The work reported here is primarily related to Portfolio C: Social fire science, Element C2: Socioeconomic aspects of fire and fuels management but is also relevant to Portfolio D: Integrated fire and fuels management research.

# Background

Record suppression costs have led to a multitude of fire cost reviews and cost studies by oversight agencies, and new rules and regulations. One of the most important and elusive issues in fire management is defining the "best" amount of fuel treatments to apply to a forested landscape. Research is developing tools and information that address a wide variety of issues related to fire suppression costs and fuels management.

**Tools have been developed to address a variety of fire suppression costs and fuels management issues.**

# Approach

Scientists have addressed several issues related to fire suppression costs: developing cost indices for gauging performance in cost containment, evaluating crew costs, developing models to optimize deployment of suppression resources, evaluating estimates of fire size and suppression costs, and developing short-term and long-term forecasts of suppression costs.

Several studies have developed models for evaluating and optimizing fuel treatments. One study incorporates fuel treatment into a stand-level model to determine planting density, timing and intensity of fuel treatment, and rotation that maximize net discounted value. The model not only includes product values and costs measured at the time of treatment but also the value of damage reduction if a fire occurs after fuel treatment. This is important because a valuation that does not include the expected value of damage reduction will underestimate the economic value of fuel treatment and distort the prioritization of fuel treatment projects. Another fuel treatment study incorporates data on forest resources, meteorology, fire occurrence, and economic impacts into a probabilistic modeling framework to build a state-of-the-science assessment of prescribed burning efficacy in Florida. The capstone analysis, applied to Volusia County in Florida, defines the optimal prescribed burning regime for a range of potential fire scenarios.

Computer analysis systems (MAGIS and MAGIS eXpress) have been developed that incorporate multiple objectives and optimize landscape level, spatial schedules of fuels treatments. MAGIS and MAGIS eXpress have been used to address trade-offs among various fuel-treatment goals for the protection of property, human life, wildlife, and hydrology. An additional project is predicting available biomass from fuel and treatments, costs to deliver this biomass to markets, and comparing net quantities of greenhouse gases and particulate matter produced if this biomass is used for energy as opposed to disposal by burning onsite and using fossil fuels to produce the equivalent useable energy.

## Products and Tools

A stratified cost index (SCI) was developed to compare the costs of large fires. The SCI is being used by the Forest Service and (tested by the Department of the Interior [DOI]) as a performance measure for suppression cost containment; by Fire Program Analysis; and is being tested for use in wildland fire decision support system (WFDSS).

MAGIS and MAGIS eXpress are "deployed" via an Rocky Mountain Research Station Web site (http://www.fs.fed.us/rm/econ/magis/).

## Results and Applications

A study of fire suppression crew costs showed that agency crews are less costly than contract crews, although agency crew costs differ widely. An assessment of the past accuracy of wildland fire situation analyses found that fire size and suppression cost estimates are systematically biased. These results have been useful in training fire managers.

A system for projecting annual suppression expenditures for the Forest Service throughout a fire season has been used by the Forest Service in meeting antideficiency regulations with regard to fire suppression expenditures and is also being implemented for the DOI agencies with fire suppression responsibilities. Procedures are being developed for making long-term suppression cost forecasts that could be used in the fire suppression budgeting process. A collaborative study of long-term climate and cost trends showed that suppression costs are closely correlated with weather conditions and that although total suppression costs have been rising in recent years, suppression costs expressed on a per-acre basis have not been increasing.

For loblolly pine (*Pinus taeda* L.) in the Southern United States, the optimal levels of fuel treatment and rotation age were found to increase as fire risk increases. The expected economic gain from fuel treatment increases with fire risk and is four times the value of the stand without fuel treatment when annual fire risk is 4 percent per year. We also evaluated two kinds of financial incentives for fuel treatment: compensating landowners for the cost of fuel treatment and requiring landowners to share the cost of fire suppression. We found that cost-sharing of fire suppression is more effective at reducing total social cost than cost sharing of fuel treatment.

A Florida study demonstrated that increasing the prescribed burning program from the current annual 4 to 5 percent of forests to 13 percent annually result in economic gains. The results also define broader policy and program implications such as (1) expanding the supply of fuel treatment services could have a great effect on managers' ability to meet goals, (2) optimal policies depend heavily on potential fire severity in addition to area, and (3) when public land managers use private sector services to prescribe burn, they drive the cost of these services higher for private forests, an unintended consequence that reduces fuels management on private lands. This study provides a methodological breakthrough and demonstrates a complete cost-benefit analysis of a fuels treatment program.

## Awards and Recognition

Chief's award for excellence in budget and financial accountability, for fire suppression forecasting, 2003.

## Principal Investigators

David E. Calkin, dcalkin@fs.fed.us: Rocky Mountain Research Station; Geoffrey Donovan, gdonovan@fs.fed.us: Pacific Northwest Research Station; Krista Gebert, kgebert@fs.fed.us: Rocky Mountain Research Station; Robert Haight; rhaight@fs.fed.us: North Central Research Station; Gregory Jones gjones@fs.fed.us; Brian Kent, bkent@fs.fed.us: Rocky Mountain Research Station; Evan Mercer, emercer@fs.fed.us; Jeffrey P. Prestemon, jprestemon@fs.fed.us: Southern Research Station

## Key Partners

Forest Service Washington office Fire and Aviation Management; Department of the Interior; Boise Wildland Fire Research and Development Unit; Scripps Institute, University of California at San Diego; University of Montana; Washington State University; National Forest Systems (regional offices and national forests)

## Funding

This research was supported by the Joint Fire Science Program, National Fire Plan Research and Development, and base research unit funding.

## Additional Readings

Amacher, G.S.; Malik, A.S.; Haight, R.G. 2005. Not getting burned: the importance of fire prevention in forest management. Land Economics. 81: 284–302.

Amacher, G.S.; Malik, A.S.; Haight, R.G. 2006. Reducing social losses from forest fires. Land Economics. 82: 367–383.

Butry, D.T.; Mercer, D.E.; Prestemon, J.P.; Pye, J.M.; Holmes, T.P. 2001. What is the price of catastrophic wildfire? Journal of Forestry. 99: 9–17.

Calkin, D.E.; Gebert, K.M.; Jones, J.G.; Neilson, R.P. 2005. Forest Service large fire area burned and suppression expenditure trends, 1970-2002. Journal of Forestry. 103(4): 179–183.

Donovan, G.H. 2005. A comparison of the costs of Forest Service and contract fire crews. Western Journal of Applied Forestry. 20(4): 233–239.

Donovan, G.H. 2006. Determining the optimal mix of federal and contract fire crews: a case study from the Pacific Northwest. Ecological Modeling. 194: 372–378.

Donovan, G.H. 2007. Comparing the cost of contract and agency fire crews. Fire Management Today. 67(1): 9–12.

Donovan, G.H.; Noordijk, P. 2005a. A comparison of wildland fire situation analysis (WFSA) predictions and actual outcomes. Fire Management Today. 65(2): 25–27.

Donovan, G.H.; Noordijk, P. 2005b. Assessing the accuracy of wildland fire situation analysis (WFSA) fire size and suppression cost estimates. Journal of Forestry. 103(1): 10–13.

**Gebert, K.M.; Calkin, D.E.; Yoder, J. 2007.** Estimating suppression expenditures for individual large wildland fires. Western Journal of Applied Forestry. 22(3): 188–196.

**Gebert, K.M.; Schuster, E.G. [In press].** Forest Service fire suppression expenditures in the Southwest. In: Narog, M.G., tech. coord. Proceedings of the 2002 fire conference on managing fire and fuels in the remaining wildlands and open spaces of the Southwestern United States. Gen. Tech. Rep. PSW-189. Albany, CA: U.S. Department of Agriculture, Forest Service, Pacific Southwest Research Station.

**Haight, R.G.; Fried, J.F. [In press].** Deploying wildland fire suppression resources with a scenario-based standard response model. INFOR: Information Systems and Operational Research.

**Hyde, K.; Jones, J.G.; Silverstein, R.; Stockmann, K.; Loeffler, D. 2006.** Integrating fuel treatments into comprehensive ecosystem management. In: Andrews, P.L.; Butler, B.W., comps. Fuels management—how to measure success: conference proceedings. Proceedings RMRS-P-41. Fort Collins, CO: U.S. Department of Agriculture, Forest Service, Rocky Mountain Research Station: 549–561.

**Jones, G.; Chew, J.; Silverstein, R.; Stalling, C.; Sullivan, J.; Troutwine, J.; Weise, D.; Gardwood, D. [In press].** Spatial analysis of fuel treatment options for chaparral on the Angeles National Forest. In: Narog, M.G., tech. coord. Proceedings of the 2002 fire conference on managing fire and fuels in the remaining wildlands and open spaces of the Southwestern United States. Gen. Tech. Rep. PSW-189. Albany, CA: U.S. Department of Agriculture, Forest Service, Pacific Southwest Research Station.

**Loeffler, D.; Calkin, D.E.; Silverstein, R.P. 2006.** Estimating volumes and costs of forest biomass in Western Montana using forest inventory and geospatial data. Forest Products Journal. 56(6): 31–37.

**Mercer, D.E.; Prestemon, J.P.; Butry, D.T.; Pye, J.M. 2007.** Evaluating alternative prescribed burning policies to reduce net economic damages from wildfire. American Journal of Agricultural Economics. 89(1): 63–77.

**Prestemon, J.P.; Mercer, D.E.; Pye, J.M.; Butry, D.T.; Holmes, T.P.; Abt, K.L. 2001.** Economically optimal wildfire intervention regimes. Paper presented at the American Agricultural Economics Association annual meeting. Chicago, IL: American Agriculture Association. 18 p.

**Prestemon, J.P.; Pye, J.M.; Butry, D.T.; Holmes, T.P.; Mercer, D.E. 2002**. Understanding broad scale wildfire risks in a human-dominated landscape. Forest Science. 48(4): 685–693.

**Silverstein, R.P.; Loeffler, D.; Jones, J.G.; Calkin, D.E.; Zuuring, H.R.; Twer, M. 2006**. Biomass utilization modeling on the Bitterroot National Forest. In: Andrews, P.L.; Butler, B.W., comps. Fuels management–how to measure success: conference proceedings. Proceedings RMRS-P-41. Fort Collins, CO: U.S. Department of Agriculture, Forest Service, Rocky Mountain Research Station: 673–688.

**Troutwine, J.M. 2005**. Forest fuel management: a spatial decision-support system developed by Rocky Mountain Research Station provides forest managers with the tools to effectively remove a build-up of fuels while adhering to principles of ecological multiple-use forest management and responding to public interests. Geospatial Solutions: 22–27.

**Zuuring, H.; Troutwine, J.M.; Jones, J.G.; Sullivan, J. 2005**. Decision support models for economically efficient integrated forest management. Proceedings: 2005 ESRI international user conference. [Place of publication unknown]: [Publisher unknown]. 22 p.

## Public Perceptions

### Highlight Contacts

Sarah McCaffrey, Northern Research Station: smccaffrey@fs.fed.us; Patricia Winter, Pacific Southwest Research Station: pwinter@fs.fed.us

### Relation to Strategic Plan

The work reported here is primarily related to Portfolio C, Element C1: Public interactions with fire and fuels management.

## Background

A critical component of the current wildland fire problem in the United States is the growing number of people living in high-fire-hazard areas. Active involvement of the public is essential to hazard reduction efforts.

## Approach

Over two dozen studies have been undertaken to better understand what shapes public views and acceptance of different fire and fuels management efforts. These studies have used a variety of methods (including onsite and mailed recreationist surveys, focus groups and workshops, telephone surveys, and mailed surveys), and been applied in diverse ecosystem and human community types across the United States, including Florida, Massachusetts, the Southwest, the Lake States, and the Rocky Mountain Region.

## Products and Tools

Results of studies can be found in Winter and Cvetkovich (2003), and on a number of Web sites: the Northern Research Station People and Fire Web site (http://www.nrs.fs.fed.us/4902/focus/people_fire/); the Fuel SAF-T project Web site (http://www.fire-saft.net/); and the Integrated Resource Solutions Web site (http://www.irsolutions.net/beta/). As part of a project to develop a suite of products and tools for planning at the project level, several documents were developed that synthesize the state of knowledge on communicating with homeowners on fuels management; aesthetics and fuels management; social acceptability of fuels treatments, and collaboration with homeowners and communities (view the Fuels Synthesis Web site: http://forest.moscowfsl.wsu.edu/fuels/publications.html). The site also includes a series of brief fact sheets for managers to assist them with interacting with the public as they plan and implement fuels treatments. In addition, a general technical report designed to provide key findings from 18 National Fire Plan research studies in a format accessible to practitioners (McCaffrey 2006), and a book with 16 articles designed to provide managers and other professionals with insight into human response to risk and how it shapes wildland fire mitigation activities (Martin et al. 2007) have been produced.

## Results and Applications

**Tools have been developed to help land managers interact with the public.**

These studies have demonstrated that fire and fuels management is a concern to individuals throughout the United States. The majority of populations studied (residents and recreationists) support thinning and prescribed burning as management tools to reduce fire risk (Hendricks et al. 2003, McCaffrey 2006). Research has found a relationship between beliefs, knowledge and familiarity with a practice, and increased support for the practice. For example, knowledge about the ecological benefits of a practice is associated with increased support, particularly for more controversial aspects such as smoke from prescribed fire (Weisshaupt et al. 2005). Trust and confidence in the implementing agency are also key factors influencing support (Absher and Vaske 2007, Martin et al. 2007). A majority of residents in fire-prone communities engage in many defensible-space activities and express support for associated recommendations (Absher and Vaske 2007, McCaffrey 2006). Although risk perception and awareness are necessary for homeowners to become active in protecting their homes, neither is a sufficient condition. Risk perception is a complex process that is shaped by individual differences in various factors including risk tolerance and perceived values at risk. The perceived effectiveness of the risk-reduction action, confidence in one's ability to perform the action, and perceived responsibility for fire management also influence readiness to take protective actions (Martin et al. 2007). No consistent evidence has been found that any specific portion of the population—whether an urban or rural resident, a new or long-term homeowner, permanent or seasonal resident, or new or experienced forest visitor—is more or less likely to understand fire risk or support a fuels management practice (Martin et al. 2007, McCaffrey 2006). Additional research is exploring whether there are variations in perceptions and attitudes for different ethnic/cultural groups (González-Cabán et al. 2007, Martin et al. 2007). Education and communication that provides clarification of how agency actions reduce fire risk and improve ecosystem health, and also addresses actions that seem inconsistent with shared values, has been shown to be essential to maintaining trust and building support (Martin et al. 2007, McCaffrey 2006). Collaboration can play a key role in establishing confidence and arriving at mutually acceptable risk reduction measures.

These findings are being used by managers to develop programs that can more effectively take into account public views and encourage proactive public participation in fire and fuels management efforts. This information has been provided to managers, fire safe councils, and other interested parties via Web sites, fuels management courses and workshops, general technical reports, meetings, and presentations. Findings from the study of Southwesterners' preferences for fire management were used in a fire managers' workshop series in the Pacific Northwest Region (Region 6).

## Principal Investigators

James Absher, jabsher@fs.fed.us; Deborah Chavez, dchavez@fs.fed.us; Armando González-Cabán, agonzalezcaban@fs.fed.us: Pacific Southwest Research Station; Pamela Jakes, pjakes@fs.fed.us; Sarah McCaffrey, smccaffrey@fs.fed.us: Northern Research Station; Carol Raish, craish@fs.fed.us: Rocky Mountain Research Station; Patricia Winter, pwinter@fs.fed.us: Pacific Southwest Research Station

## Key Partners

California Polytechnic State University, San Luis Obispo; Colorado State University; Michigan State University; Pennsylvania State University; University of Arizona; University of Florida; University of Massachusetts; University of Minnesota; Washington State University; Western Washington University

## Funding

Supported by the National Fire Plan and the Joint Fire Science Program.

## Literature Cited

**Absher, J.D.; Vaske, J.J. 2007**. Modeling public support for wildland fire policy. In: Reynolds, K.M.; Thompson, A.J.; Köhl, M.; Shannon, M.A.; Ray, D.; Rennolls, K., eds. Sustainable forestry: from monitoring and modeling to knowledge management and policy science. Wallingford, United Kingdom: CABI International: 159–170. Chapter 9.

**González-Cabán, A.; Loomis, J.B.; Rodriguez, A.; Hesseln, H. 2007**. A comparison of CVM response rates, protests, and willingness to pay of Native Americans and general population for fuels reduction policies. Journal of Forest Economics. 13: 49–71.

**Hendricks, W.; Chavez, D.; Phippen, K. 2003**. Observance-influence of fire management and place attachment at Big Sur. In: Jakes, P.J., comp. Homeowners, communities, and wildfire: science findings from the National Fire Plan: proceedings of the 9th international symposium on society and resource management. Gen. Tech. Rep. NC-231. St. Paul, MN: U.S. Department of Agriculture, Forest Service, North Central Research Station: 45–54.

**Martin, W.E.; Raish, C.; Kent, B., eds. 2007**. Wildfire risk: human perceptions and management implications. Washington, DC: Resources for the future.

**McCaffrey, S., tech. ed. 2006**. The public and wildland fire management: social science findings for managers. Gen. Tech. Rep. NRS-1. Newtown Square, PA: U.S. Department of Agriculture, Forest Service, Northern Research Station. 202 p.

**Weisshaupt, B.R.; Carroll, M.S.; Blatner, K.A.; Robinson, W.D.; Jakes, P.J. 2005**. Acceptability of smoke from prescribed forest burning in the northern inland West: a focus group approach. Journal of Forestry. 103(4): 189–193.

**Winter, P.L.; Cvetkovich, G.T. 2003.** A study of Southwesterners' opinions on the management of wildland and wilderness fires: fire management version. www.wildfirelessons.net/documents/SDSU_tech_02_fire_FMO_eversion.pdf. (April 2007).

# Additional Readings

**Cvetkovich, G.T.; Winter, P.L. 2007.** The what, how, and when of social reliance and cooperative risk management. In: Siegrist, M.; Earle, T.C.; Gutscher, H., eds. Trust in cooperative risk management: uncertainty and skepticism in the public mind. London: Earthscan: 187–209.

**Daniel, T.C.; Carroll, M.S.; Moseley, C.; Raish, C., eds. 2007.** People, fire, and forests: a synthesis of wildfire social science. Corvallis, OR: Oregon State University Press. 226 p.

**González-Cabán, A.; Loomis, J.B.; Bair, L.S. 2003.** Forest fire reduction policies in Florida: comparison between English- and Spanish-speaking households. In: Galley, K.E.M.; Klinger, R.C.; Sugihara, N.G., eds. Proceedings of fire conference 2000: the 1st national congress on fire ecology, prevention, and management. Misc. Publ. 13. Tallahassee, FL: Tall Timbers Research Station: 124–131.

**Loomis, J.; Ellingson, L.; González-Cabán, A.; Seidl, A. 2006.** The role of ethnicity and language in contingent valuation analysis: a fire prevention policy application. American Journal of Economics and Sociology. 65(3): 559–586.

**Martin, I.M.; Bender, H.; Raish, C. [In press].** What motivates individuals to protect themselves from risks: the case of wildland fires. Risk Analysis.

**McCaffrey, S. 2004.** Thinking of wildfire as a natural hazard. Society and Natural Resources. 17(6): 509–516.

**Monroe, M.C.; Pennisi, L.; McCaffrey, S.; Mileti, D. 2005.** Social science to improve fuels management: a synthesis of research related to communicating with the public on fuels management efforts. Gen. Tech. Rep. GTR-NC-267. St. Paul, MN: U.S. Department of Agriculture, Forest Service, North Central Research Station. 42 p.

**Nelson, K.C.; Monroe, M.C.; Johnson, J.F.; Bowers, A. 2004.** Living with fire: homeowner assessment of landscape values and defensible space in Minnesota and Florida, USA. International Journal of Wildland Fire. 13(4): 413–425.

**Raish, C.; González-Cabán, A.; Condie, C.J. 2005.** The importance of traditional fire use and management practices for contemporary land managers in the American Southwest. Environmental Hazards. 6: 115–122.

**Toman, E.; Shindler, B.; Brunson, M. 2006.** Fire and fuel management communication strategies: citizen evaluations of agency outreach activities. Society and Natural Resources. 19: 321–336.

**Vaske, J.J.; Absher, J.D. [In press].** Predicting homeowners' defensible space behavior intentions. Human Ecology Review.

**Vaske, J.J.; Absher, J.D.; Bright, A.D. [In press].** Salient value similarity, social trust and attitudes toward wildland fire management strategies. In: Burns, R., comp., ed. Proceedings of the 2006 Northeastern recreation research symposium. Newtown Square, PA: U.S. Department of Agriculture, Forest Service, Northeastern Research Station.

**Vogt, C.; Winter, G.; Fried, J.S. 2005.** Predicting homeowners' approval of fuel management at the wildland-urban interface using the theory of reasoned action. Society and Natural Resources. 18: 337–354.

# Strategic and Tactical Fuel Treatment Evaluation Tools

## Highlight Contact

Ken Skog, Forest Products Laboratory: kskog@fs.fed.us

## Relation to Strategic Plan

The work reported here supports objectives in Portfolio C: Social fire science, Element C3: Organizational effectiveness; Portfolio D: Integrated fire and fuels management research, Element D3: Biomass utilization, product development and forest operations associated with fire and fuels management activities; and Portfolio E: Develop and deliver knowledge and tools to policymakers, wildland fire managers, and communities, Element E1: Synthesis and tool development.

# Background

Strategic identification and local placement of fuel treatments are significant regional and local forest management problems addressed by two tools developed by Forest Service Research and Development.

# Approach

The two tools described below were developed by teams composed of Forest Service and university research scientists and national forest experts. Specialist contributed expertise on silvicultural systems, fire hazard and fire hazard reduction, forest inventory data, harvesting systems and harvest cost estimation, economic evaluation, mathematical modeling, and Web-based modeling.

# Products and Tools

Fuel Treatment Evaluator (FTE) 3.0 (Miles et al. 2006) is a Web-based tool that helps analysts identify forest areas in the West with high fire hazard, simulate alternative thinning treatments to meet hazard reduction targets, and estimate kinds and amounts of wood biomass removed and costs of removal (Skog et al. 2006). The tool addresses the key problem of identifying locations where biomass removals could cover the costs of thinning treatments to reduce hazard (see fig. 1).

My Fuel Treatment Planner (myFTP) (Fight 2006) is a user friendly tool that assists managers in estimating costs, net revenues, economic effects, and surface fuels associated with various fuel reduction treatments. The spreadsheet application

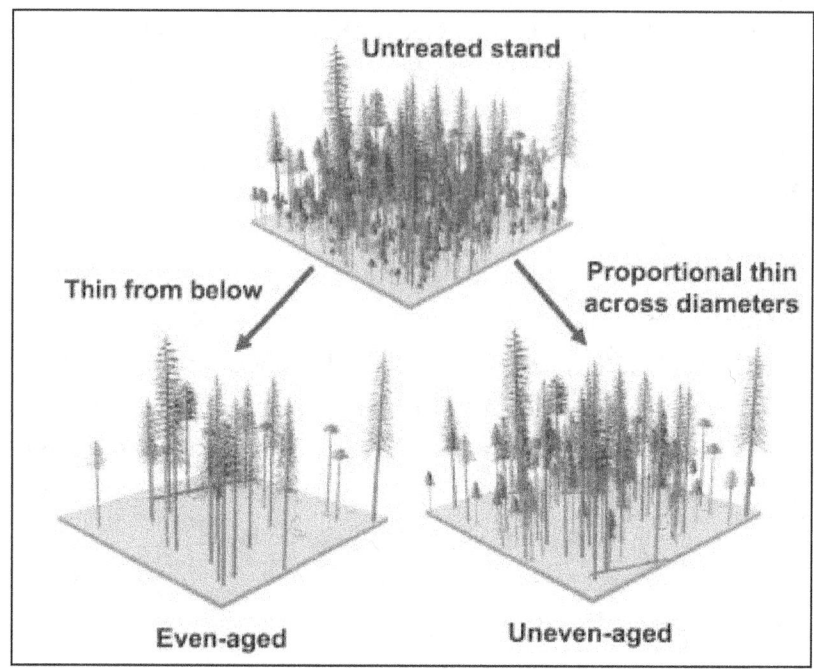

Figure 1—Forest treatment alternatives used by the Fuel Treatment Evaluator 3.0.

is simple to use yet based on years of data. MyFTP provides insights on how to think through economic analyses and interacts compatibly with existing planning tools (see fig. 2).

## Results and Applications

The FTE 3.0 has been used to identify opportunities for using wood biomass from thinnings to generate electric power (1) across the Western United States for the Western Governors Association (Skog and Barbour 2006) and (2) in parts of Oregon for the Oregon Forest Resources Institute (OFRI 2006).

MyFTP has been incorporated into the analytical process for the FIRESHED program, which is used for all Forest Service fire hazard reduction projects in California, is being piloted at 10 other locations around the Western United States, is now available for general use, and has been incorporated into national training required for fuel specialist certification.

## Principal Investigators

Ken Skog, kskog@fs.fed.us: Forest Products Laboratory; Jamie Barbour, jbarbour01@fs.fed.us, Roger Fight (now retired): Pacific Northwest Research

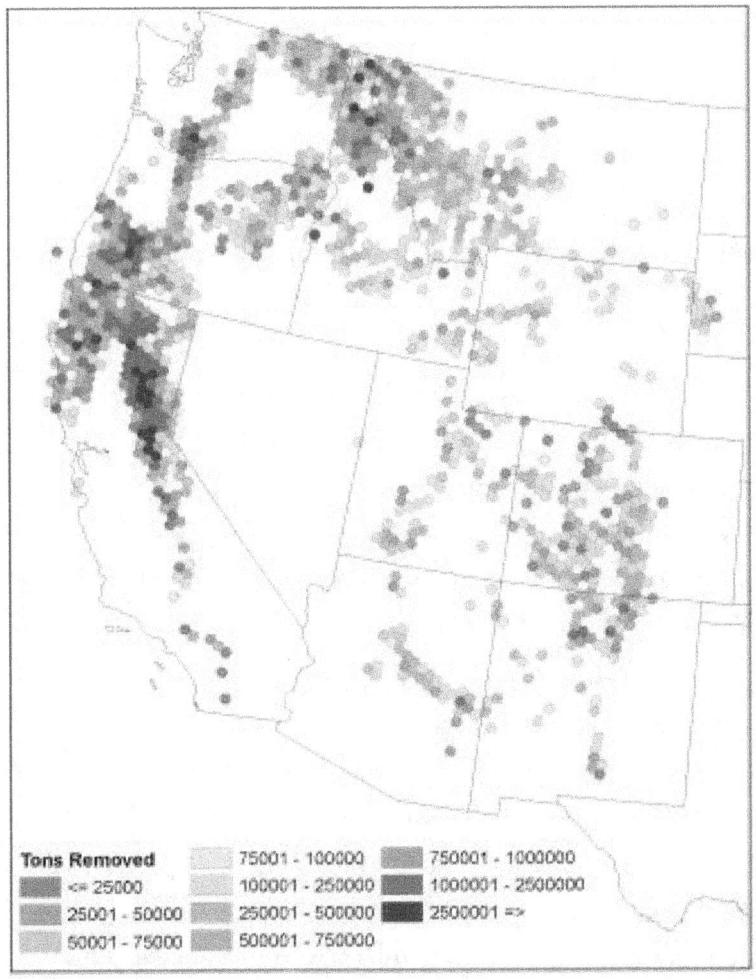

Figure 2—Biomass removed (oven dry tons) from simulated thinnings by 160,000-acre hexagon for uneven-age fuel-hazard-reduction treatments.

Station; Karen Abt, kabt@fs.fed.us: Southern Research Station; Ted Bilek, tbilek@fs.fed.us: Forest Products Laboratory; Bobby Hugget, rhuggett@fs.fed.us: Southern Research Station; Pat Miles, pmiles@fs.fed.us: Northern Research Station; Elizabeth Reinhardt, ereinhardt@fs.fed.us; Wayne Shepperd, wshepperd@fs.fed.us: Rocky Mountain Research Station

## Key Partners

Forest Management, Washington office, Forest Service; Clean and Diversified Energy Advisory Committee for the Western Governors Association (WGA report); Mason, Bruce & Girard, Inc. (Oregon Forest Resources Institute report);

National Forest System: Pacific Northwest Region (Region 6); Northern Region (Region 1); University of Washington Stand Management Cooperative; University of California, Davis

## Funding

This research was supported by National Fire Plan Research and Development.

## Literature Cited

**Fight, R. 2006.** My fuel treatment planner. [Web site with software and guide-book]. http://www.fs.fed.us/pnw/data/myftp/myftp_home.htm. (May 2007).

**Miles, P.D.; Skog, K.E.; Huggett, R.J. 2006.** Fuel treatment evaluator 3.0. [Web-based analysis tool]. http://ncrs2.fs.fed.us/4801/fiadb/fire_tabler_us/rpa_fuel_reduction_treatment_opp.htm. http://www.ncrs2.fs.fed.us/4801/fiadb/FTE_Version3/WC_FTE_version3.asp. (May 2007).

**Oregon Forest Resources Institute [OFRI]. 2006.** Biomass energy and biofuels from Oregon's forests. Portland, OR. [Roger Lord prepared chapter 2: Assessment of potential using the Fuel Treatment Evaluator 3.0 Web analysis tool]. http://www.oregonforests.org/media/pdf/Biomass_Full_Report.pdf. (May 2007).

**Skog, K.E.; Barbour, R.J. 2006.** Forest fuel treatment & thinning biomass–timberland. In: Western Governors Association. 2006 biomass taskforce report: supply addendum. Denver, CO: 11-12ff. http://www.westgov.org/wga/initiatives/cdeac/Biomass-supply.pdf. (May 2007).

**Skog, K.E.; Barbour, R.J.; Abt, K.L.; Bilek, E.M.; Burch, F.; Fight, R.D.; Hugget, R.J.; Miles, P.D.; Reinhardt, E.D.; Shepperd, W.D. 2006.** Evaluation of silvicultural treatments and biomass use for reducing fire hazard in Western States. Res. Pap. FPL-RP-634. Madison, WI: U.S. Department of Agriculture, Forest Service, Forest Products Laboratory. 29 p. http://www.fpl.fs.fed.us/documnts/fplrp/fpl_rp634.pdf. (May 2007).

## Additional Reading

**Biesecker, R.L.; Fight, R.D. 2006.** My fuel treatment planner: a user guide. Gen. Tech. Rep. PNW-GTR-663. Portland, OR: U.S. Department of Agriculture, Forest Service, Pacific Northwest Research Station. 31 p. http://www.fs.fed.us/pnw/pubs/pnw_gtr663.pdf. (May 2007).

# Understand the Wildland-Urban Interface

## Highlight Contact

Susan Stewart, Northern Research Station: sistewart@fs.fed.us

## Relation to Strategic Plan

This work supports objectives in Portfolio C, Element C2: Socioeconomic aspects of fire and fuels management.

## Background

The wildland-urban interface (WUI) is where houses and dense vegetation are both present. With few limits on where homes are built, housing now extends across suburban and rural landscapes, and the most intense development pressure is felt in forested areas. These housing trends have serious implications for wildfire suppression costs, public safety, and fire ecology. Understanding the WUI provides the foundation for quantifying wildland fire risks and prioritizing treatments.

**Understanding the WUI helps quantify fire risks and prioritize treatments.**

## Approach

Based on the Federal Register definition of the WUI, housing (census) and land cover (National Land Cover Datasets) data were combined in a geographical information system (GIS) to identify census blocks with at least low-density housing (>6.17 housing units/km$^2$, or >1 housing unit per 40 acres) and wildland vegetation (>50 percent of pixels). Where housing met the threshold but vegetation was less dense, portions of census blocks were included when they fell within 2.4 km (1.5 mi) of dense wildland vegetation (>75 percent) (fig. 3). Rectifying 1990 and 2000 census blocks allowed subcounty analysis of WUI growth (Hammer et al. 2007).

Based on the WUI's location and growth, work can begin to assess the relative fire hazards facing residential areas across the country and target high-hazard neighborhoods with the information, outreach, resource management, and regulations needed to mitigate wildland fire danger. Regional data sets detailing biophysical conditions have been used to assess the WUI fire hazard in portions of California, Michigan, Oregon, Washington, and Utah; as Landfire data become available, this analysis can be extended nationally.

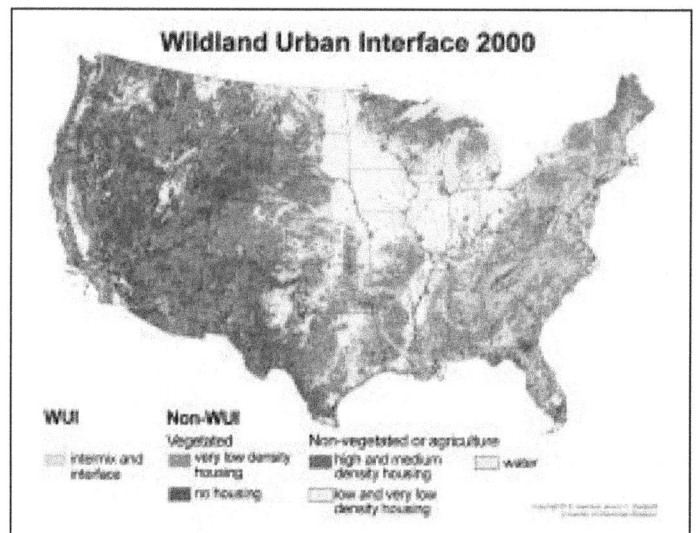

Figure 3—The 2000 wildland-urban interface.

In Puerto Rico, satellite (Landsat TM) and population (census) data were combined to classify land use and identify the WUI, the suburban and exurban residential areas with forest or grassland vegetation (fig. 4). Fuel loads and fire danger zones were also identified.

## Products and Tools

At http://silvis.forest.wisc.edu/projects/WUI_Main.asp, users can download WUI and housing density maps and data for states and Forest Service regions in the lower 48 States. The WUI data also support other tools, such as the Fuel Treatment Evaluator developed by Miles et al. 2006, and a Web site where homeowners can assess their property's WUI status and fire hazard, at http://firecenter.berkeley.edu/toolkit/. Maps of Puerto Rico's WUI, fuel loads, and fire danger zones are available through the Forest Service International Institute of Tropical Forestry.

## Results and Applications

The WUI in 2000 encompassed 37 percent of U.S. homes (Radeloff et al. 2005). All states in the lower 48 had some WUI, and in 19 states, it includes more than half of all homes. The booming housing market of the 1990s added 8.2 million housing units, 60 percent of all new homes, to the WUI. In northern lower Michigan, 25 percent of the WUI faces relatively high fire hazard and over 88 percent of the WUI with high fire hazard has low housing density (<1 housing unit per 2 ha or

Figure 4—Wildland-urban interface in Puerto Rico.

5 ac) (Haight et al. 2004, fig. 5); in southern California's shrublands, the interactions between human presence and fire-prone ecosystems has increased ignitions and threatens to change ecosystem characteristics. Analysis of housing growth and fire regime condition class in California, Oregon, and Washington found there were nearly 1.5 million WUI housing units in areas with 0- to 35-year fire-return intervals and 3.4 million in areas with 35- to 100+ year fire-return intervals (Hammer et al. 2007). In both fire regimes, most WUI housing units (66 percent and 90 percent, respectively) are in areas with a current condition outside the historical range of variability.

As in the continental United States, the WUI covers one-third of the land area in Puerto Rico (Martinuzzi et al. 2007). The vast majority of wildland fires in Puerto Rico are human-induced and these increasingly occur within the WUI or in protected areas bordering it. Each year, an estimated 3,000 to 6,000 wildland fires occur in Puerto Rico. Their ecological effects are compounded by high species diversity, a high number of endemic species, extensive landscape fragmentation, vulnerability to drought, and high levels of human use of the landscape, particularly in the WUI. This analysis helps fire managers better define fire risks and management priorities for Puerto Rico.

Wildland-urban interface research has found a wide community of users, from technicians developing geographic information system data layers for community or regional plans, to policymakers interested in the scope of the WUI problem, to popular media covering wildland fire.

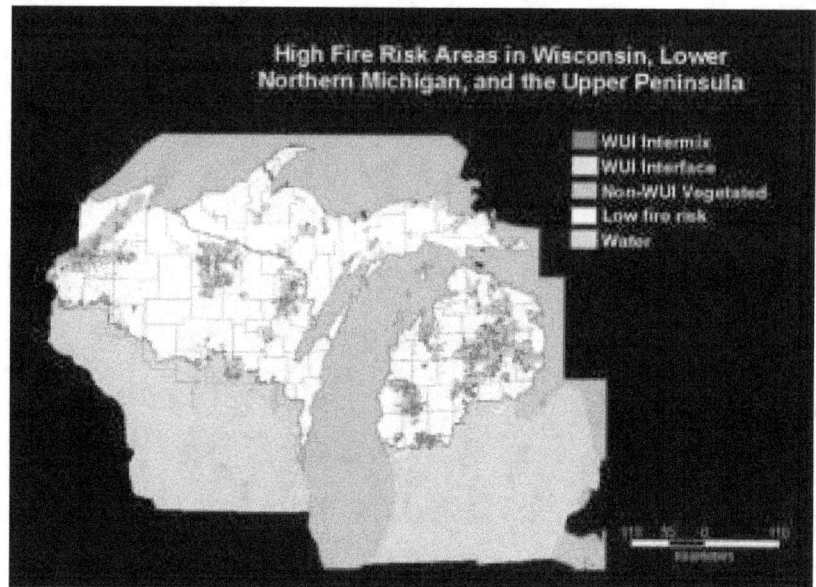

Figure 5—High fire risk areas in Wisconsin, Lower Northern Michigan, and the Upper Peninsula.

## Literature Cited

**Haight, R.G.; Cleland, D.T.; Hammer, R.B.; Radeloff, V.C.; Rupp, T.S. 2004.** Assessing fire risk in the wildland urban interface. Journal of Forestry. 102(7): 41–48.

**Hammer, R.B.; Radeloff, V.C.; Fried, J.S.; Stewart, S.I. 2007.** Wildland urban interface growth during the 1990s in California, Oregon and Washington. International Journal of Wildland Fire. 16: 255–265.

**Martinuzzi, S.; Gould, W.A.; Ramos Gonzalez, O.M. 2007.** Land development, land use, and urban sprawl in Puerto Rico: integrating remote sensing and population census data. Landscape and Urban Planning. 79: 288–297.

**Miles, P.D.; Skog, K.E.; Huggett, R.J. 2006.** Fuel treatment evaluator 3.0. [Web-based analysis tool]. http://ncrs2.fs.fed.us/4801/fiadb/fire_tabler_us/ rpa_fuel_reduction_treatment_opp.htm. http://www.ncrs2.fs.fed.us/4801/fiadb/ FTE_Version3/WC_FTE_version3.asp. (May 2007).

**Radeloff, V.C.; Hammer, R.B.; Stewart, S.I.; Fried, J.S.; Holcomb, S.S.; McKeefry, J.F. 2005.** The wildland urban interface in the United States. Ecological Applications. 15(3): 799–805.

# Fire Social Science Research–Next Steps

Richard W. Haynes, Sarah McCaffrey, and Jeff Prestemon

## Discussion

Since 2000, National Fire Plan funding has allowed fire social science research to expand significantly. Much has been learned about the social and economic issues connected with wildland fire and fuels management. The highlights illustrate the breath of social fire-science work that has taken place in Forest Service Research and Development as well as a range of research outcomes including tools that can be used to solve a variety of problems. This focus on developing tools useful to managers has been one of the hallmarks of work with the fire community where research outputs are denominated in descriptions of tools that were placed in managers hands. The highlights illustrate a variety of tools from the wildland urban interface maps to software or other computer-based "decision support tools."

The concept of "tools" can be painted with a broader brush to include not only computer software, but also other forms of checklists, inventories, guidelines, and templates based on research and that serve the needs of fire management. Such tools expand the range of opportunities for mutual and constructive interaction among researchers, managers and the public. If we extend the concept of tools to include "means" of various types to achieve one or more "ends," then we can identify field-related outputs of research in terms of consultations, workshops, seminars, and other forms of training and education as forms of "tools" to support fire or other management operations.

The information developed to date is being used to enhance the ability of agencies and communities to meet land management objectives in an effective and efficient manner that is well informed by public needs and preferences and contributes to a broader understanding of key public values and concerns about fire and fuels management—before, during, and after wildland fires and fuels treatments; social and economic effects of different fire and fuels management decisions; external and internal barriers to effective fire management; and effect of existing and proposed policies on management options and decision space. The research will also provide guidelines and tools for effective and efficient communication, both externally and internally; improving safety, reliability, and ability to meet management objectives; working with communities and other partners to achieve fire and fuels management goals; and assessing tradeoffs in economic, ecological, and quality-of-life values of different decision options.

Although much has been learned, there are still many areas where research can continue to contribute to improved fire management. Below we identify these future research needs. Each of these needs is characterized by an array of products that include scholarly research, syntheses, and tools for the user community. With regard to priorities, we suggest that more resources be directed toward the organizational effectiveness element. We recognize that such shifts need to be made incrementally.

# Future Research Directions

## C1-Public Interactions

**Public perception and trust—**
There is a need to expand research on the dynamics of trust, how trust interacts with fire and fuels management actions and the agencies taking such actions, and how trust manifests across a greater variety of ethnic, cultural, and economic groups to determine how these groups accept and are affected by fire and fuel management programs.

- What are the consequences of alternative "social contracts" (i.e., the expectations that communities or individuals might have that public agencies will protect them) for fire management? Does the shift of the Forest Service to becoming a fire management agency break its "social contract" with the American public as a conservation agency, and are there new suppression approaches (e.g., appropriate management response) that challenge the existing social contract?
- Do the basic tenets of trust building and trust retention (for example, honesty, credibility, and fairness) hold in the arena of fire management, or does the public demand something different from wildland fire managing agencies?

**Collaboration and planning—**
There is a need to improve our understanding of the barriers placed by the public (or the market) on effective fuel management and fire suppression activities.

What are the primary decision considerations in implementing prescribed fire at the wilderness/nonwilderness interface to both support wilderness resource benefits and protect nonwilderness values?

What are the trends in public attitudes toward wildland fire use for resource benefits outside of wilderness, and what are the societal or physical influences on these attitudes?

**Communication—**

There is a need to identify public information needs before, during, and after fires and fuel treatment activities, especially prescribed burning, and the form of dissemination that best serves fire and fuels management decisionmaking. We need to develop tools that help integrate social, economic, risk and uncertainty information into fire and fuels management decisionmaking processes.

# C2-Socioeconomic Effects

**Impacts of wildland fire and fuels management—**

There is a need to develop frameworks that enable managers to identify and quantify the short- and long-term socioeconomic impacts of fire and fuels management on people, communities, markets and natural resources, including their temporal and distributional effects.

- What decision frameworks will aid fire management in mixed-ownership situations? Do private homeowners respond to larger social objectives (e.g., firefighter safety and restoration of fire on public lands) when improving fire resistance of their private lands?
- What are the social impacts of decisions made during wildland fire? Are there alternative decision frameworks that minimize these impacts while maintaining citizen and firefighter safety? What influences their decisions to leave or stay?

**Costs and benefits of fire and fuels management—**

There is a need to develop frameworks to support evaluations of the market and nonmarket benefits associated with fire and fuels management (fire suppression, hazardous fuels reduction, use of wildland fire and restoration work).

- What methods are available to reduce fire suppression costs that are socially acceptable and achievable (recognizing values saved and lost from fire suppression)?
- Are suppression costs commensurate with the values at risk?

There is a need to develop methods to represent better the values at risk that the agency is attempting to protect.

- What are the methodological and empirical issues that need to be understood?
- How can measures of values at risk be made operational?

There is a need for tools that managers can use for evaluating fire management alternatives.

- How can managers analyze the efficiency and equity effects of fire suppression and fuels management?
- How can managers improve their understanding of methods to reduce human-caused wildland fire? Such methods will need to build on understanding the social, economic, and biophysical underpinnings of human-started fires, and the implications of human-started fires for changes in aggregate wildland fire activity, values at risk, fuels management, fire prevention efforts, and wildland fire suppression expenditures.
- What tools can be developed to improve engagement with communities and other partners in fire suppression and prevention and for dealing with safety and public health concerns associated with fire?

## C3-Organizational Effectiveness

**Organizational issues—**
There is a need to improve the understanding and knowledge of how organizational structures and institutional incentives and disincentives impact the effectiveness and efficiency of fire and fuels management organizations.

- What are the temporal, spatial, budgetary, economic, and social impacts and tradeoffs among alternative fuels management, prevention, detection, suppression, and postfire rehabilitation strategies?
- What is the role and effect of incentives and disincentives on fire management decisionmaking? How are changes in individual manager's personal incentive structures affecting decisionmaking? What are the impacts of regulatory changes (i.e., the new air quality regulations and others) on fire management decisions?

**Personal and situational issues—**

There is a need to develop assessments of how the perception of and attitudes about risk of fire personnel impact fire and fuels management decisions, what factors affect perceptions of risk, and how these perceptions differ within the agency, and with the public.

- How do the agencies train the emerging fire decisionmakers given their differences in experience, education, values, perceptions of environmental factors (like global climate change), aversion to risk, and trust in organizational objectives?

## Metric Equivalents

| When you know: | Multiply by: | To get: |
| --- | --- | --- |
| Acres | 0.405 | Hectares |
| Tons | .907 | Tonnes |
| Cubic feet | .0283 | Cubic meters |
| Miles | 1.609 | Kilometers |
| Square miles | 2.59 | Square kilometers |